Liber Lunæ

BOOK OF THE MOON

Sepher ha-Levanah

By Don Karr and Stephen Skinner

Sepher Raziel: Liber Salomonis, a 1564 English Grimoire from Sloane MS 3826
Singapore: Golden Hoard Press, 2010

Online works by Don Karr

BIBLIOGRAPHIC SURVEYS
http://www.digital-brilliance.com/contributed/Karr/Biblios/index.php
- Notes on the Study of *Merkabah* Mysticism and *Hekhalot* Literature in English
  with an appendix on Jewish Magic
  - Notes on Editions of *Sefer Yetzirah* on English
    - Notes on the Study of Early Kabbalah in English
      - Notes on the *Zohar* in English
    - Notes on the Study of Later Kabbalah in English:
      - The Safed Period & Lurianic Kabbalah
      - The Study of Christian Cabala in English

KNOTS & SPIRALS:
http://www.digital-brilliance.com/contributed/Karr/KS/index.php
- Notes on the Emergence of Christian Cabala

SOLOMONIC MAGIC
http://www.digital-brilliance.com/contributed/Karr/Solomon/index.php
- British Library Sloane MS 3826
- The Study of Solomonic Magic in English

SELECTED WRITINGS OF FRANCISCUS MERCURIUS VON HELMONT
http://www.digital-brilliance.com/contributed/Karr/VanHelmont/index.php
- *A Cabbalistical Dialogue*
- *The Paradoxal Discourses*: CHAPTER IV
- AN APPENDIX OF SEVERAL QUESTIONS WITH THEIR ANSWERS CONCERNING THE
  HYPOTHESIS OF THE REVOLUTION OF HUMAN SOULS
  from *The Divine Being and Its Attributes*
  - *Seder Olam*

HEKHALOT RABBATI
translated from the Hebrew & Aramaic by Morton Smith,
corrected by Gershom Scholem, transcribed and edited with notes by Don Karr
http://www.digital-brilliance.com/contributed/Karr/HekRab/index.php

THE KABBALAH OF MAAT
http://www.digital-brilliance.com/contributed/Karr/Maat/index.php
- Approaching the Kabbalah of Maat: Altered Trees and the Procession of the Æons
  - Methods of Maat: Sources for the Kabbalah of a Future Æon

Selected Writings of OAI (Ordo Adeptorum Invisiblum) & 416

Other Books in the Source Works of Ceremonial Magic series:

Volume I – The Practical Angel Magic of John Dee's Enochian Tables - ISBN 978-0-9547639-0-9

Volume II – The Keys to the Gateway of Magic: Summoning the Solomonic Archangels & Demonic Princes – ISBN 978-0-9547639-1-6

Volume III – The Goetia of Dr Rudd: The Angels & Demons of *Liber Malorum Spirituum seu Goetia* – ISBN 978-0-9547639-2-3

Volume IV – The Veritable Key of Solomon – 978-0-7378-1453-0 (cloth) ISBN 978-0-9547639-8-5 (limited leather edition)

Volume V – The Grimoire of Saint Cyprian: *Clavis Inferni* - ISBN 978-0-9557387-1-5 (cloth edition) – ISBN 978-0-9557387-4-6 (limited leather edition)

Volume VI – *Sepher Raziel: Liber Salomonis,* a 1564 grimoire – ISBN 978-0-9557387-3-9 (cloth edition) – ISBN 978-0-9557387-5-3 (limited leather edition)

Volume VII – *The Book of the Moon: Liber Lunae & Sepher ha-Levanah* – ISBN 978-0-9568285-2-1 (cloth edition) – ISBN 978-0-9568285-3-8 (limited leather edition)

Volume VIII – The Magical Treatise of Solomon: the *Hygromanteia* – 978-0-9568285-0-7 (cloth edition) – ISBN 978-0-9568285-1-4 (limited leather edition). The Greek source of the *Key of Solomon.*

For further details of forthcoming volumes in this series edited from classic magical manuscripts see www.GoldenHoard.com

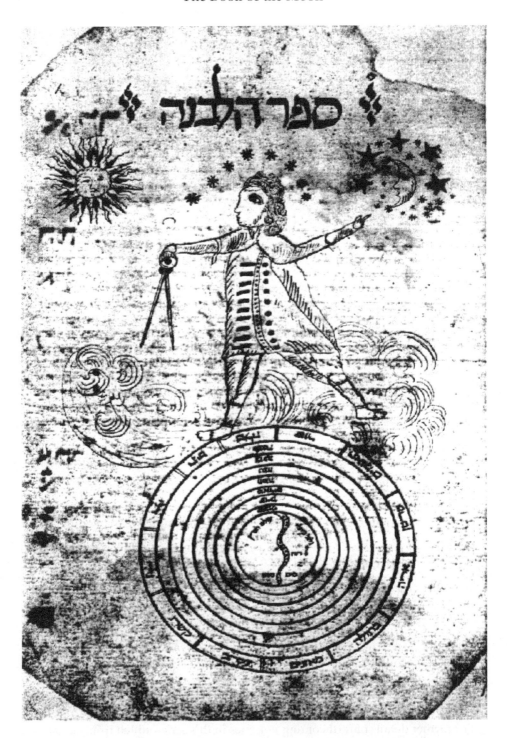

Title page of *Sepher ha-Levanah* from British Library Oriental MS 6360.

Book of the Moon

OR

Liber Lunæ

being British Library Sloane MS 3826, *fols.* 57-83v, 84-96v
transcribed, annotated, and introduced
with a contemporary English version

by Don Karr

together with a facsimile of A. W. Greenup's edition of

Sepher ha-Levanah

from Oriental MS 6360, with an English translation

by Calanit Nachshon

Foreword

by Stephen Skinner

GOLDEN HOARD PRESS

2017

Published by Golden Hoard Press Pte Ltd
PO Box 1073 Robinson Road
Singapore 902123
SINGAPORE

www.GoldenHoard.com

Second Edition

ISBN 978-1-912212019

Printed by CreateSpace

To the memory of my mother
Winifred Louise Whitcomb Karr
(1918-2010)

ACKNOWLEDGEMENTS

My thanks to Sears R. Jayne of Brown University, who originally provided the microfilm of British Library Sloane MS 3826 in 1978; to Arthur Versluis of Michigan State University, who saw to the publication of my initial online edition of *Liber Lunæ* in *Esoterica*, VOLUME III: § ARCHIVES, in 2001 [www.esoteric.msu.edu/]; to Colin Low, who maintains the website HERMETIC KABBALAH and, since 2003, has been the host of the working version of *Liber Lunæ*, along with many of my other transcriptions and papers [www.digital-brilliance.com/index.php]; to Christopher Warnock, Esq., author and creator of the website RENAISSANCE ASTROLOGY [www.renaissanceastrology.com/index.html], who provided invaluable comments and suggestions during the composition of the introduction; to Sharon Horowitz, who administered access to A. W. Greenup's edition of *Sepher ha-Levanah* from the collections of the Hebraic Section, African and Middle Eastern Division, Library of Congress, Washington, D. C; and to the Trustees of the British Library for permission to reproduce the folio from Oriental MS 6360.

CONTENTS

TABLES AND FIGURES

FOREWORD

The significance of this volume in the series *Source Works of Ceremonial Magic* is that it addresses the *other* magical tradition that concerns itself with talismans, sigils, and the 28 Mansions of the Moon, like the *Picatrix*. It is also significant for the history of magic in that it shows two very similar, almost parallel texts, one in Latin and one from the Hebrew magical tradition.

Like Don Karr's previous volume *Sepher Raziel*, it points up the importance for magic of 'suffumigations' or incense. These are not just used to 'set the scene' but are an important and essential ingredient in the processes of invocation and evocation, as 'spiritual creatures,' be they angels, daemons, spirits, demons, and even gods, respond directly to the correct use of incense. It is no coincidence that where paganism is still practiced as a living religion, predominantly in Asia (rather than as a reconstructed revival, as in Europe) detailed attention is paid to the burning of substances that will either attract or dispel the gods and the spirits. The practice of burning things like 'Hell banknotes' during the hungry ghost festival in Chinese areas is widespread. Whatever you think about its effectiveness from the point of view of the recently departed, the concept that burning enables you to pass something from this world to the other is never questioned. Hence the burning of incense, of the right kind, is also able to affect the denizens of the other world. *Sepher Raziel* is very specific in this respect.

Another concern that many magical texts have, and which is pointed up in the present text, is the correct selection of times for magical rituals. Just as we wouldn't expect success if we visited a bank at 3am in the morning, so the calling of 'spiritual creatures' should be done at the correct time, to maximize the chances of success. This applies not only to the time of the lunar month (as marked out by the 28 Mansions of the Moon) but also the correct day of the week (as determined by the ruling planet) and the correct time of the day (as marked out by the planetary hours).

In all, this volume fills in some of the gaps that are to be found in many grimoires. Note that three extra last minute pages have been inserted after page 64 without adjusting the subsequent pagination.

Stephen Skinner
Singapore, September, 2011

INTRODUCTION

LIBER LUNÆ APPEARS on folio leaves 84-96v of British Library Sloane MS 3826 within a bound manuscript collection titled *Liber Salomonis*, also called *Cephar Raziel* (i.e., *Sepher Raziel*), which is also taken as the name of the first work in the collection. Sloane MS 3826 is a sixteenth-century English translation of a collection of older Latin texts.[1]

Liber Lunæ is itself a composite of four sections:

1. THE MANSIONS OF THE MOON: a preamble with general instructions [*fols.* 84-84v] in the name of Hermes [*fol.* 84], followed by descriptions of the twenty-eight mansions of the Moon, where they fall in the cycle of the zodiac, and what their names and virtues are [*fols.* 84v-86v]. Within this section [*fol.* 84v], Bolemus (a variant of Belenus) is cited, presumably drawing on the authority of his *De Imaginum Lunæ*. Reference to Aristotle appears on *fol.* 86.[2]

2. SUFFUMIGATIONS [*fol.* 86v] and the fifty-five angels with their bindings and workings [*fols.* 86v-87].

3. THE HOURS OF THE DAY AND NIGHT: operations of the twelve hours of the day [*fols.* 87-89v] and the twelve hours of the night [*fols.* 90-92v], along with four operations for day or night [*fols.* 92v-93]. In this section, Bolemus is cited three times [*fols.* 87, 90, and 90v]; *fol.* 90 also mentions "Salomon."

4. THE FIGURES OF THE PLANETS: figures (i.e., magic squares) of the planets (Saturn, Jupiter, Mars, Sun, Venus, Mercury, and Luna) with their operations and virtues [*fols.* 93-96v].[3] MAGICAL INSCRIPTIONS: *annuli* (RINGS) [*fol.* 96v], *sigilli* (SYMBOLS) and images [*fol.* 97].

---

[1] For a summary of the different types of "Raziel" material and the contents of British Library Sloane MS 3826, refer to *Sepher Raziel: Liber Salomonis*, edited by Don Karr and Stephen Skinner (Singapore: Golden Hoard Press, 2010): especially Skinner's "Foreword," pages 13-23, and my "Introduction to the Manuscript," pages 45-47.

[2] Distinction might be drawn between the titles *Liber Lunæ* and *Liber imaginum Lunæ* when used in their strictest sense. *Liber Lunæ* often refers to texts on the twenty-eight mansions of the Moon, their portions of the zodiac, and their names and virtues, i.e., what is represented in both *Liber Lunæ* and *Sepher ha-Levanah*. *Liber imaginum Lunæ* might omit the astrological details but include instructions on the construction of talismanic images, words to utter, and suffumigations (as in the second section of *Picatrix*, BOOK IV, CHAPTER 9). This said, however, combinations or conflations of the two can use either title but most often come under the title *Liber Lunæ*.

[3] Note that four of the magic squares in the Sloane *Liber Lunæ*—Sun, Venus, Mercury, and Luna—contain mistakes, which have been rectified in the present edition.

PRINTED NOTICES OF *LIBER LUNÆ*

• Arthur Edward Waite, giving an account of the *Liber Salomonis* MS, writes,

> The independent treatises which follow the *Sepher Raziel* in Sloane MS 3826 extract matter from the *Sworn Book* [of Honorius], while that entitled *Liber Lunæ*, concerning the intelligences of the mansions of the moon, the squares of the planets, their seals, rings, and so forth — which, by the way, seems in this form unknown to modern critics — has given material to other and later collections.[1]

• Lynn Thorndike describes *Liber Lunæ*[2] as a book

> of the twenty-eight mansions and twenty-eight images of the moon and the fifty-four[3] angels who serve these images. And as Albert [i.e., Albertus Magnus, c.1200-1280] spoke of a treatise of magic illusions which accompanied the seven books of necromantic images for the planets, so this *Liber lune* is itself also called *Mercury's magic illusion*. It probably is the same *Book of Images of the Moon* which William of Auvergne [Bishop of Paris, 1180-1249] described as attempting to work magic by the names of God.[4]

• In his dissertation, *Religion, Science, and the Transformations of Magic: Manuscripts of Magic 1300-1600*[5], Frank Klaassen determines two streams of magic in texts prior to 1500. The first stream is "epitomized by certain texts of Arabic image magic" (page 2); works of this type include Thebit ibn Qurra's *De imaginibus* (10th century), *De imaginibus* of Belenus, and, I would hasten to add, significant portions of the compendious *Picatrix* (11th century). The second stream is ritual magic, whose texts "employ complex Christian ritual and are, very much, the progeny of the liturgy and Christian religious sensibilities" (page 3); this category would include works of "necromancy" and "notary art." While Klaassen's portrayal of ritual magic may be true of the later grimoires[6], it is not true of the majority of European works of ritual

---

[1] *Book of Ceremonial Magic Including the Rites and Mysteries of Goetic Theurgy, Sorcery and Infernal Necromancy* (London: William Rider, 1911, reprinted frequently), page 23.

[2] Thorndike notes Corpus Christi MS 125, *fols.* 62-68 (Corpus Christi College, Cambridge) and Digby 228, *fols.* 54v-55v (Bodleian Library, Oxford).

[3] Our *Liber Lunæ* states [*fol.* 86v], "And thou shalt exercise in all the hower of suffumigacion aswell in the works of good as of evill by 55 angells." The list of angels which follows this statement, however, contains fifty-one names.

[4] *A History of Magic and Experimental Science*, VOLUME II (New York / London: Columbia University Press, 1923), page 223.

[5] University of Toronto, 1999.

[6] On the most important cycle of the late grimoires, refer to my article, 'The Study of Solomonic Magic in English' in *Sepher Raziel*, edited by Don Karr and Stephen Skinner.

magic prior to 1500, which retain a remarkable amount of non-Christian, even pre-Christian, substance.[1] Also, it would be more accurate for Klaassen to use the term *nigromancy*, the evocation of demons, rather than *necromancy*, the evocation of the dead.[2]

Klaassen refers to two *Liber Lunæ* manuscripts: British Library Harley MS 80, ff. 77v-81r ("the most complete version of this text which I have seen" page 80, note 8) and Bodleian Library Digby MS 228 ("a late fourteenth-century codex"). While Klaassen lists *Liber Lunæ* among texts of image magic (on pages 40-41), he later deliberates as to whether it might belong "under the umbrella of necromantic[3] magic" (page 85). Klaassen echoes these points in his paper, "English Manuscripts of Magic, 1300-1500: A Preliminary Survey,"[4] where, in a discussion of *Liber Lunæ* as it appears in Digby 228, he offers the following summary:

> *Liber lune* (*sic*) is a work of Arabic image magic attributed to Hermes. The magical effects sought for are often of bad intent, ranging from binding someone's tongue, to twisting a man's limbs, to destroying an entire region. The instructions concern engraving images as the moon moves through its houses[5], and the magical processes involve the reciting of angel names and suffumigations. To distinguish this text from the works of necromancy[6] on the basis of content would be difficult. We have a complex array of ethereal beings, we have images and we have incantations. The ritual features of the process receive a considerable amount of attention.

The Sloane MS 3826 *Liber Lunæ* refers to a number of the mansions as "evill" (*fol.* 84v *ff*), and speaks of "worchings of evill and tribulation and destruction" (*fol.* 85v), of the "bynding of tongs" and of the destruction of "howses townes cityes and divers tents" (*fol.* 90v), and so on. However, our manuscript's terse section on the mansions of the Moon lacks instructions on images, angel names, and suffumigations.[7]

---

[1] Refer to the first three volumes of Lynn Thorndike's *History of Magic and Experimental Science*.

[2] The term *nigromancy*, which literally means "black divination," is itself problematic, for it strongly suggests summoning the evil denizens of hell. It has commonly – albeit erroneously – been supplanted by the term *necromancy* since the Middle Ages.

[3] Read "nigromantic."

[4] In *Conjuring Spirits: Texts and Traditions of Medieval Ritual Magic*, edited by Claire Fanger (University Park: Pennsylvania State University Press, 1998), pages 11-14.

[5] The choice of the word "Houses" (rather than "Mansions") is very misleading given the use of the term to refer to the divisions of a horoscope.

[6] Read "nigromancy."

[7] These instructions do not appear in *Sepher ha-Levanah* either.

In his dissertation (page 80), Klaassen speculates,

> The text of *De imaginibus* of Belenus [called in Sloane MS 3826 "Bolemus"] is, in fact, closely related to the *Liber lune* and may derive from it. I would argue that the *Liber lune* probably came first.

Throughout our version of *Liber Lunæ*, Belenus is cited (as *Bolemus* – and, as we shall see below, throughout *Sepher ha-Levanah* as כאלינוס, *Kelinos*). On the face of it, this suggests that *De imaginibus* is the source of *Liber Lunæ* rather than the other way around. However, we find that Belenus is quoted within a more general citation of Hermes. Then, in another text on the lunar mansions, we find Hermes quoted within a citation of Aristotle with no mention of Belenus. Elsewhere, we find references to Solomon, Ptolemy, Thebit ibn Qurra, and "the second Pliny," along with "old wise men" and "the wise of India" — a jumble of plausible attribution, pseudepigraphy, and anachronism. We will take up the problem of origins more broadly below.[1]

• Benedek Láng notes three early references to *Liber Lunæ*[2]:

- William of Auvergne (ca. 1180-1249), Bishop of Paris, who wanted "to defend the licit and innocent scientific literature from the contaminating proximity of necromantic works,"[3] mentions *Liber Lunæ* along with a handful of other "technical-operative works on Hermetic magic"[4] in *De universo* (1231-1236).

- "a short enigmatic treatise" somewhat similar to William's *De universo*, "but [which] goes further in tolerance."[5] Among the books which were "falsely considered necromantic" and "contain the great secrets of the ancient philosophers"[6] are listed "the title and incipit of Hermes' *Liber Lunæ*, the *Liber de imaginibus diei et noctis* ('The Book on the Images of Day and Night') of Belenus, and *Liber runarum* ('The Book of Runes')."[7]

- the handbook of Egidius of Corintia copied in 1488 which "introduces a number of book titles as belonging to *nigromantia*, *magica*, and *naturalia*" (*ibid*), including, among others, *Clavicula Salomonis*, *Liber Semphoras*, *Liber institutionis Raziel*, *Liber Almandel*, and *Liber Lunæ*.[8]

---

[1] In § TEXTS RELATED TO *LIBER LUNÆ*.
[2] *Unlocked Books: Manuscripts of Learned Magic in the Medieval Libraries of Central Europe* University Park: Pennsylvania State University Press, 2008.
[3] Lang, page 24.
[4] Page 26.
[5] Page 32.
[6] Ibid.
[7] Page 33.
[8] Page 34.

SEPHER HA–LEVANAH

The title *Sepher ha-Levanah* (ספר הלבנה, lit. BOOK OF THE MOON) represents any of a number of Hebrew versions of *Liber Lunæ*. Fabrizio Lelli writes,

> Mention of this text [i.e., *Sepher ha-Levanah*] in several works of Jewish authors from Spain, along with the testimony of Abraham of Esquira's *Sefer Yesod 'Olam*, suggests that some versions of the *Book of the Moon* and its Arabic original circulated in medieval Spain. Linguistic features of the Hebrew versions show that at least three of them were translated from Arabic.[1]

Moshe Idel discusses the influence of magic on the Castilian kabbalists of the late thirteenth century, mentioning in particular "the Arabic text known in Latin under the title *Picatrix*." Idel continues,

> Another Hermetic treatise, the Book of the Moon, *Sefer ha-Levanah*, had considerable impact at the same time, and was quoted by three Kabbalists in the late thirteenth and early fourteenth centuries—[1] R. Moshe ben Nahman, Nahmanides, and, under the latter's influence, [2] R. Bahia ben Asher ... and early in the fourteenth century, [3] R. Abraham of Esquira. Later on, in late fifteenth century, a fourth Kabbalist, R. Yohanan Alemanno was familiar with another version of the book.[2]

Lelli notes that the eclectic Alemanno (1435-1500?) copied "one of the longest versions of the *Book of the Moon*" as part of his pursuit of 'Hebrew *Hermetica*.'[3] Regarding Alemanno's version of *Sepher ha-Levanah*, Klaus Herrmann cites—then mildly refutes—a conjecture in Lelli's 1990 article from *Henoch* 12:

> Having compared the extant versions of the work on magic, *Sefer ha-Levanah*, Fabrizio Lelli, referring precisely to the textual version found in Alemanno's untitled work, comes to the following conclusion:
>
> > "è estramente difficile, in mancanza di un'edizione critica, avventurarsi in ipotesi premature sulla tradizione del testo di questo opusculo. Un esame più approfondo e un confronto con la tradizione greca, araba e Latina potrebbero permettere di ricostruire la formazione di queste tradizioni ebraiche."
>
> > "[I]t is extremely difficult, in the absence of a critical edition, to venture [what

---

[1] 'Hermes among the Jews: *Hermetica* as *Hebraica*: From Antiquity to the Renaissance,' in *Magic, Ritual, and Witchcraft*, Volume 2, Number 2, Philadelphia: University of Pennsylvania Press, Winter 2007; page 127.

[2] "On European Cultural Renaissances and Jewish Mysticism, see *Kabbalah: Journal for the Study of Jewish Mystical Texts*, VOLUME 13, edited by Daniel Abrams and Avraham Elqayam (Los Angeles: Cherub Press, 2005).

[3] 'Hermes among the Jews,' page 127.

would be] a premature hypothesis regarding the traditions within this little book. A deeper examination and comparison with the Greek, Arabic and Latin traditions could permit us to reconstruct the framework of the Hebrew traditions [it may incorporate]".[1]

Looking at Alemanno's version of this work, we can say with all probable certainty that the explanation for most of the textual variants lies not in the Greek, Arabic or Latin translations, but solely in Alemanno's discriminatory linguistic sense.[2]

One of the *Sepher ha-Levanah* manuscripts was "edited, for the first time, by A. W. Greenup" (London: 1912).[3] As with our *Liber Lunæ*, Greenup's *Sepher ha-Levanah* is introduced "under the name of הרמס [Hermes]" and offers "directions for preparing צלמים [*tzelemim* - images] in accordance with various positions of the moon" (Greenup's INTRODUCTION). Greenup's edition also accords with the Sloane *Liber Lunæ* in containing sections on the names and images of the hours of the day and night, and two paragraphs about potions (or *suffumigations*) to be used for good and evil images respectively.[4] In fact, Greenup's text contains only two brief passages which are not in some way paralleled in our *Liber Lunæ*: three paragraphs in § (5),[5] "the first explaining that every מזל [*mazel*[6] – fortune, i.e., sun-sign] can be divided into three equal portions; the second giving the signs of the zodiac; and the third beginning פנים צומח [lit. face growing]"[7] (Greenup's INTRODUCTION), and a statement at the end lauding the "images by *Petolmeo* [Ptolemy]."[8]

Joseph Peterson notes[9] that the MS of *Sepher ha-Levanah* which Greenup used (British Library Oriental MS 6360) "is in fact part of a larger work which had

[1] My thanks to Melissa Tassi for translating the Lelli passage, which originally appeared in 'Le versioni ebraiche di un testo ermetico: il Sefer ha-levanah,' in *Henoch* 12, (Torino: Marietti Editori, 1990), page 163.

[2] Herrmann's paper, The Reception of Hekhalot-Literature in Yohanan Alemanno's Autograph MS Paris 849,' is part of *Studies in Jewish Manuscripts*, edited by Joseph Dan and Klaus Herrmann (Tübingen: Mohr Siebeck, 1999); the passage quoted is on page 74.

[3] Given below is a full facsimile of Greenup's edition with an English translation by Calanit Nachshon, which I have annotated and introduced.

[4] Greenup's description of *Sepher ha-Levanah* § (3) is quite misleading. See my introduction to the translation below.

[5] Fol. 4 *a*.

[6] The plural, *mazloth*, refers to the zodiac. The second part of the MS which contains *Sepher ha-Levanah* is called *Sepher Peuloth ha-Mazloth*, Book of the Operations of the Zodiac.

[7] A 'face' is the 10-degree division of each sign of the zodiac. Agrippa refers to the faces in connection with the *decans*.

[8] Fol. 6 *b*.

[9] At TWILIT GROTTO—ESOTERIC ARCHIVES, article "A. W. Greenup: Sefer ha-Levanah—The Book of the Moon," at www.esotericarchives.com/levanah/levanah.htm .

become separated," namely, *Sepher Mafteah Shelomoh* (BOOK OF THE KEY OF SOLOMON—Oriental MS 14759). *Sepher ha-Levanah* is not actually part of the *Sepher Mafteah Shelomoh* material per se but rather was combined with it, even as our *Liber Lunæ* was bound with *Sepher Raziel* in *Liber Salomonis*.[1]

For our purposes, all that needs to be established is that *Sepher ha-Levanah*, far from embodying a long-lost ancient Hebrew original of this material, reproduces Arabic, Latin, and perhaps Greek sources in Hebrew translation. Specifically, Greenup's *Sepher ha-Levanah* is derived from a late Medieval Latin version of *Liber Lunæ* which is very similar in content, form, and detail to the English translation in Sloane MS 3826, which is also from a Latin version. Both Greenup's Hebrew *Sepher ha-Levanah* and the English *Liber Lunæ* of Sloane MS 3826 are products of the sixteenth century.

TEXTS RELATED TO *LIBER LUNÆ*

Much of the lore preserved in *Liber Lunæ* has existed for thousands of years and, in various forms, has found a wide circulation. The major sections of *Liber Lunæ*, THE MANSIONS OF THE MOON, THE HOURS OF THE DAY AND NIGHT, and THE FIGURES OF THE PLANETS, contain material which is similar to that found in other compendia of magic.

There is some confusion as to whether the *Liber Lunæ* material came to the Greek Hermetica from Arabic sources or the other way around. In *Jewish Translation History: A Bibliography of Bibliographies and Studies*,[2] Robert Sangerman describes *Liber lune* as "a Latin text derived from Arabic sources traceable to the Hellenistic tradition known as the Corpus Hermeticum." Indeed, among the Greek magical papyri (2nd century BCE—5th century CE) are fragments correlating types of spells and the positions of the Moon through the zodiac, as in *PGM* III. 275-81 [Horoscope] and *PGM* VII. 284-99 [orbit of the moon].[3]

To take the issue just one step further, Charles Burnett notes that "…we have reasonable evidence that at least part of the Arabic Hermetica derived from Persian and ultimately Indian sources" ('Arabic, Greek, and Latin Works on Astrological Magic Attributed to Aristotle,' page 87, cited below).

---

[1] Refer to *Sepher Maphteah Shelomoh – Book of the Key of Solomon: An Exact Facsimile of an Original Book of Magic in Hebrew*, edited by Hermann Gollancz (York Beach: The Teitan Press, 2008), which reproduces Gollancz' 1903 and 1914 publications on the Hebrew *Key*; see especially Stephen Skinner's foreword.

[2] Amsterdam – Philadelphia: John Benjamins B.V., 2002, page 81.

[3] See Hans Dieter Betz, *The Greek Magical Papyri in Translation*, VOLUME ONE: TEXTS, second edition (Chicago – London: University of Chicago Press, 1992), pages 26 and 124.

§1. THE MANSIONS OF THE MOON

Traditions surrounding the mansions of the Moon are based on the correlation of the Moon and an annual cycle of twenty-seven or, more often, twenty-eight small constellations of fixed stars which constitute a 'lunar zodiac.' These traditions are ancient and far-reaching, appearing variously as the twenty-seven Vedic *nakshatras*, the twenty-eight Chinese *hsiu*, and the twenty-eight Arabic *manāzil al-kamar*, literally MANSIONS OF THE MOON, which are apparently derived from the Greek *Hermetica*.[1]

The twenty-eight constellations of this sequence are of unequal size, and the Moon's rotation against that of the solar year effects some slippage. Thus, in order to take "a more Platonic approach that saw the regular, even harmony of the Tropical Mansions as reflecting the perfection of higher spiritual realities,"[2] late antique and medieval Arabic and European astrologers fixed the mansions into the *tropical* zodiac, that is, the regular cycle of sun-signs — this despite the awkwardness of twenty-eight being set against twelve, which lines up only at the equinoxes and solstices (i.e., the first, eighth, fifteenth, and twenty-second mansions commence simultaneously with Aries, Cancer, Libra and Capricorn, respectively).

In "Arabic, Greek, and Latin Works on Astrological Magic Attributed to Aristotle,"[3] Charles Burnett discusses Latin and Arabic manuscripts treating the lunar mansions under the name of Aristotle (who is mentioned in the Sloane *Liber Lunæ, fol.* 86r). The most complete of these manuscripts is the *Hidden Book* quoted in *Kitāb al-Ustuwwatās*, in which

> all twenty-eight mansions of the moon are included, and the larger work into which the text is incorporated gives detailed instructions on how to make up the talismans, and what secret names to use to summon the angels, or the spiritual forces, of the planets.[4]

This *Hidden Book* purports to have been prepared by Aristotle for the young

---

[1] The Greek system was recorded by Dorotheus of Sidon (1st century CE), whose *Pentateuch* (lit. *Five Books*) on Hellenistic astrology came to be known primarily through their Arabic translation from around 800 CE. See David Pingree, 'Māshā' Allāh: Some Sasanian and Syriac Sources,' in *Essays on Islamic Philosophy and Science*, edited by George Fadio Hourani (Albany: State University of New York Press, 1975).

[2] Christopher Warnock, "Mansions of the Moon in Astrology & Magic," specifically § "Tropical versus Constellational Mansions," at the RENAISSANCE ASTROLOGY website: www.renaissanceastrology.com/mansionsmoon.html.

[3] In *Magic and Divination in the Middle Ages*, Aldershot: Variorum, 1996.

[4] Burnett, page 84.

Alexander of Macedon, who would become Alexander the Great (356-323 BCE). It was subsequently put into Arabic, and possibly Syriac,

> by the greatest of the Baghdādī translators, Hunain ibn Ishāq (c. 809-[8]73 A. D.). It was taken from its context and abbreviated in Arabic. At some stage in its transmission it lost its second half. The abbreviated and truncated version was translated into Latin—and possibly Greek …[1]

Results of the *Hidden Book*'s being "abbreviated" and "truncated" appear in two other manuscripts which Burnett discusses and attaches to his article as APPENDICES I and II. His APPENDIX III offers a parallel from the more complete version, which opens, "Aristotle said," although the real matter of the text commences with "Hermes said."

Burnett's appendices in more detail:

I. Pseudo-Aristotle, *De Luna* (in Latin) derived from two MSS, noting, "The translations of the names of the lunar mansions [from the Arabic] are found only in [version] L[2] but are virtually the same, as far as they go, as those found in Agrippa von Nettesheim, *De occulta philosophia*, II, chapter 33." *De Luna* covers the first fourteen mansions.

II. The Lunar Mansions in the *Kitāb al-bulhān* (Bodleian, Oriental 133, fol. 270— translated into English) with a plate of images from this MS on page 97. This MS also contains the first fourteen mansions.

III. An example of the Lunar Mansions from the *Hidden Book* as quoted in *Kitāb al-Ustuwwatās*.[3] This excerpt covers the first two mansions.

The mansions section of *Liber Lunæ* in Sloane MS 3826 is itself "abbreviated," giving the names and virtues of the mansions but providing nothing on the construction of their corresponding talisman images, secret utterances, or other details. Our *Liber Lunæ* does not even include all twenty-eight mansions: Through an error by the copyist or an omission in his source, the third mansion is missing.

The Arabic *Picatrix*, or *Ghayat al-hakim* (GOAL OF THE WISE, ca. 1050 CE) BOOK I, CHAPTER 4, systematically enumerates the twenty-eight mansions of the Moon according to "the wise of India" with regard to making talismans. The names of the mansions in *Picatrix* indicate that the corresponding names in *Liber Lunæ*, i.e., 1. *Meliatalh*, 2. *Albutaim*, 3. (missing), 4. *Aldeboran*, etc., are variations (or corruptions) of their Arabic counterparts: 1. THE HOUSE OF AL-

---

[1] Burnett, page 85.
[2] = P. Liechtenstein, *Sacratissime astronomie Ptholemei liber diversarum rerum* (Venice, 1509) fols 13r-13v.
[3] Paris, Bibliothèque Nationale, ar. 2577, fol. 241 – translated into English.

SHARATAIN, or *Alnath*, 2. THE HOUSE OF AL-BOTEIN, or *Albotain*, 3. THE HOUSE OF AL-THURAYYA, or *Azoraya*, 4. THE HOUSE OF AL-DEBARAN, or *Aldebaran*, etc.

In each example, the title of the mansion cited first in SMALL CAPS is from the Ouroboros *Picatrix...* VOLUME 1;[1] which is almost unique in using the word "house" rather than "mansion" — an unfortunate choice given the use of the term "house" elsewhere in astrology[2]. This is followed by the name of the mansion in *italics* as it appears in the Adocentyn *Picatrix*.[3]

The manners of defining the periods of the mansions in *Picatrix* and *Liber Lunæ* differ, even while both use the *tropical* zodiac. *Picatrix* sets out the signs, degrees, minutes, and seconds of each. For example, the description of the first mansion begins, "It starts at the beginning of the ♈ position to 12°, 51', 26" from it." *Liber Lunæ* generally uses a planetary rulership scheme "based on the Chaldean order,"[4] i.e., Saturn, Jupiter, Mars, Sun, Venus, Mercury, Moon, cycling continuously in this order.[5] For example, "...when *Meliatalh* that is Luna in the first mansion that is the face of martis [Mars]...." However, *Liber Lunæ* often defines a mansion by its portion of the zodiac, as in the second mansion, "*Albutaim* that is the wombe of Ariets [= the middle of Aries]." *Liber Lunæ* frequently gives both. (Refer to *Table 1.*) Also, where *Picatrix* provides a paragraph (at least five lines) on each mansion, *Liber Lunæ* offers a clipped line or two.

BOOK 4, CHAPTER 9 of the Adocentyn Press *Picatrix*, which is "based primarily on David Pingree's critical edition of the Latin translation made at the court of Alfonso the Wise of Castile in 1256," appends "the 28 Mansions of the Moon according to the second Pliny,"[6] which enumerates the mansions, their virtues, and the names of their lords, giving directions on the materials and images for their talismans along with words to utter over these. The names for the mansions in this BOOK 4, CHAPTER 9 are, for the most part, variations of the names given in *Picatrix*, BOOK 1, CHAPTER 4. However, this content on the construction of the talismans within the cycle of lunar mansions does not

---

[1] *Picatrix: Ghayat al Hakim, The Goal of the Wise*, translated from the Arabic by Hashem Atallah, edited by William Kiesel, Seattle: Ouroboros Press, 2000, pp. 19-20.

[2] As noted above, Frank Klaassen also misleadingly refers to the mansions as "houses."

[3] *Picatrix: The Classic Medieval Handbook of Astrological Magic*, translated by John Michael Greer and Christopher Warnock, Iowa City: Adocentyn Press, 2010, pp.32-33.

[4] Christopher Warnock, comments of September 8, 2010.

[5] See Christopher Warnock's "Planetary Hours & Days Main Page," INTRODUCTION, at www.renaissanceastrology.com/planetaryhoursarticle.html

[6] INTRODUCTION, page 18.

appear in VOLUME 2 of the Ouroboros *Picatrix*,[1] where the composition of BOOK 4, CHAPTER 9 matches Martin Plessner's description of the Arabic *Picatrix*, reproduced by Joseph Peterson at *Twilit Grotto*[2]:

> Chapter 9 deals, in its entirety, with descriptions of talismans, which expressly depend on the virtues [*or* qualities]. Astrological material is not mentioned. The objects of the talismans are of different kinds: for drugs, for attracting or repelling animals, producing color effects etc.

Relying on *Picatrix*, Heinrich Cornelius Agrippa (1486-1535) includes "Of the twenty-eight mansions of the Moon and their virtues" as CHAPTER XXXIII of *The Second Book of Occult Philosophy, or Magic*, following this with CHAPTER XLVI, "Of the images of the mansions of the Moon," and, in *The Third Book*, CHAPTER XXIV, "On the names."[3]

British Library Harley MS 6482, a late seventeenth-century manuscript volume from a set of six called "The Treatises of Dr Rudd,"[4] also includes "Of the 28 Mansions of the Moon and Their Strength and Virtue in Mundane Affairs" and "Of the Images of the Mansions of the Moon," both drawn from Agrippa's *Second Book*.[5]

Unlike Agrippa and at least one version of *Picatrix*, our *Liber Lunæ* does not include an "Of the images..." section or, for that matter, an account of the

---

[1] Translated from the Arabic by Hashem Atallah and Geylan Holmquest, edited by William Kiesel, Seattle: Ouroboros Press, 2008.

[2] "Picatrix...," at www.esotericarchives.com/picatrix.htm. The description quoted originally appeared in *"Picatrix": Das Ziel des Weisen, von Pseudo-Maǧǧrītī*, translated into German from the Arabic by Hellmut Ritter and Martin Plessner. London: Warburg Institute, University of London, 1962, page lxxv.

[3] These can be found in Donald Tyson's edition of Agrippa's *Three Books of Occult Philosophy* (St. Paul: Llewellyn Publications, 1993), pages 368-370, 392-393, and 533 respectively.

[4] "They seem not to be originals but rather copies made by a certain Peter Smart in the period 1699-1714" (McLean's INTRODUCTION to *A Treatise on Angel Magic*, page 9).

Material from Harley MS 6482, namely *Janus Magica Reserata*, *Nine Hierarchies*, and *Nine Celestial Keys*, also appears in *The Keys to the Gateway of Magic: Summoning the Solomonic Archangels and Demon Princes*, edited by Stephen Skinner and David Rankine (Singapore: Golden Hoard Press, 2005). Harley MS 6483, Dr Rudd's version of the *Lemegeton*, has also been published as *The Goetia of Dr Rudd*, edited by Stephen Skinner and David Rankine (Singapore: Golden Hoard Press, 2007).

Agrippa's sections on the mansions of the Moon were also copied by Francis Barrett in *The Magus* (London: 1801); see Barrett's BOOK I, PART II, CHAPTERS XXXIII and XLIV, and BOOK II, PART I, CHAPTER XI.

[5] *A Treatise on Angel Magic, being a complete transcription of Ms. Harley 6482 in the British Library*, edited by Adam McLean, pages 127-134.Grand Rapids: Phanes Press, 1990.

twenty-eight angels. Elsewhere within Sloane MS 3826, however, there is material which supplements *Liber Lunæ*'s MANSIONS, namely *fols.* 80-83v, where parts of the zodiac, functions, images and materials for talismans, and words to say are given. A transcription of this section appears below in § SUPPLEMENTARY MATERIAL.

Comparisons between *Liber Lunæ* and other sources treating the mansions of the Moon can be quite efficiently made by referring to Stephen Skinner's expansion of Aleister Crowley's *Liber 777, The Complete Magician's Tables.*[1] Tables H39 through H42 are drawn from "the list of Mansions of the Moon given by Haly Abenragel [*or* 'Alî ibn abi 'r-Rijâl] circa 1000 AD, in the Latin translation of the book by Abenragel called *Libri de Judiciis Astorum,* [*summa cura ... latinitati donati,*] *per Antonium Stupam,* published in Basel in 1551 [by Henricus Petrus]," providing both the "Indian Interpretation" (H41) and the "Dorotheos Interpretation" (H42) of the mansions' indications. Tables H43-H44 set out the mansions of the Moon and their virtues according to Agrippa's *Second Book;* Tables H45-H46 list the magical objectives and methods for the images of the mansions. On either side of the tables just mentioned reside columns outlining the "Mansions of the Moon – Hindu *Nakshatras*" (H37-H38) and "The Mansions of the Moon – Chinese *Hsiu*" (H47-H53).[2]

---

[1] Singapore: Golden Hoard Press, 2006.

[2] For more on the Mansions of the Moon, refer to the wealth of information on RENAISSANCE ASTROLOGY at www.renaissanceastrology.com/index.html (© 2000-2009, Christopher Warnock), starting with "The Mansions of the Moon in Astrology & Magic" at www.renaissanceastrology.com/mansionsmoon.html. To delve further, see Christopher Warnock's book, *The Mansions of the Moon: A Lunar Zodiac for Astrology and Magic,* illustrated by Nigel Jackson (Iowa City: Renaissance Astrology, 2010), available at www.renaissanceastrology.com/astrologyandmagicbooks.html.

Liber Lunæ

Table 1

THE XXVIII MANSIONS OF THE MOON[60]

MAN-SION	PART OF THE YEAR	FACE	NAME	INDICATIONS IN BRIEF
1		face of Martis	*Meliatalh*	separation
2	wombe of Ariets		*Albutaim*	joining together
3[61]	head of Taurus		*Aqhoranay/ Altuayib*	words of grace, joining together
4	eye of Taurus	evil face of Mercury	*Aldeboran*	adversity
5		evil face of Luna	*Almaycen*	allegation, building
6		facies Saturni	*Althaya*	love
7	end of Geminory	face of Jovis	*Addiraen*	wild beasts, concord
8	head of Cancer	face of Martis	*Innatar*	ships and floods
9	wombe of Cancer		*Alkaud*	fowls and culvers
10	end of Cancer and beginning of Leo	face of Venus	*Algeibh*	wolves, foxes, and wild beasts
11	hart of Leo	black face of Mercury	*Azobra/ Azumble*	separations, allegations, binding infirmities
12	Cauda leonis and caput virginis	face of Luna	*Algapha*	conjunction, shaping
13	wombe of Virgo	face of Saturn	*Alans*	conjunction, shaping, joining together
14	the end of Virgo	good face of Jovis	*Alchumech*	inclination, love and dilection
15	head of Libra	evil face of Martis	*Algarst*	tribulation, destruction
16	middle of Libra	evil face of Solis	*Azubene*	destruction, allegation, impediment, letting
17	the end of Libra and beginning of Scorpio	evil face of Venus	*Alichul*	good, tribulation and impediment
18	part of Scorpio	face of Mercury	*Alcox*	good, binding of tongues
19	Scorpio Caudey and head of Sagittary	face of Luna	*Alhebus*	fornication, sedition, allegation, lust
20	wombe of Sagittary	face of Saturn	*Anahim*	incisation of love, concord
21	end of Sagittary	face of Jovis	*Alberda*	Silence
22	head of Capricorni		*Ceadaebyh*	desolation, discord, separation

---

[60] *Liber Lunæ*, fols. 84v-86v:
[61] *Liber Lunæ* omits the third mansion. In order to complete the table, the PART OF THE YEAR, NAME, and INDICATIONS from the third mansion of *Sepher ha-Levanah* are included here.

MAN-SION	PART OF THE YEAR	FACE	NAME	INDICATIONS IN BRIEF
23	hart of Capricorni	face of Solis	*Azatalbuta*	"him that swoloweth," good
24	Cauda Capricorni and head of Aquarius		*Zadac Zahond*	Good
25	wombe of Aquarius		*Cealaghbrah*	Silence
26	end of Aquarius and head of Pisces	face of Luna	*Alfgarem*	recuperations, inclination, dilection, love
27	wombe of Pisces	face of Saturni	*Alfgagir*	separations, departing, binding of infirmities
28	cauda pisces / face of Jovis		*Albecten*	good, profit

§ 3. THE HOURS OF THE DAY AND NIGHT

Establishing names and images for the hours of the day and night grew from traditions begun in Egypt in the third millennium BCE. Priests determined a "system for dividing the night into a series of equal parts ... to be able, mentally and ritually, to accompany the Sun-god *Re* along the different stages of his dangerous nightly journey through the dark regions, the abode of the dead, of gods and spirits."[62] In one such system, the names of the twelve hourly positions indicate parts of the body of *Nut*, through which *Re* passes each night; these thus serve as mnemonic devices for the ritual.[63]

> As they were an integral part of Egyptian religion it is not astonishing that the hours, named and personified, should have been one of the elements ... that entwined with ideas and beliefs from Græco-Roman religion after the conquest of Alexander (332 BC), to produce the syncretic mixture which characterized Hellenistic devotion.[64]

Such *personifications* were adapted to the prevailing pantheon, as, for example, in *The Hygromanteia of Solomon* of the early Byzantine period, which gives the Greek names of the planetary gods, along with "the Moon," and occasionally "the Sun" instead of Helios, in rotation for the hours of each day and night of the week, commencing with the ruler associated with that day, i.e., the Sun for Sunday, the Moon for Monday, etc. The rotation, using the initial cycle for Sunday as an example, runs the Sun (or Helios), Aphrodite, Hermes, the Moon, Kronos, Zeus, Ares, Helios, Aphrodite, etc. The *Hygromanteia* also gives an imposing list of the angels *and* demons for all of the hours of all seven days, commencing with the archangel associated with each day, i.e., Michael, Gabriel, Samouel, Ouriel, Raphael, Agathouel, and Sabapiel.[65]

Systems of names for the hours complementary to their ruling gods developed among the ancient Greeks. Maddison and Turner note Hyginus

---

[62] Francis Maddison and Anthony Turner, 'The Names and Faces of the Hours,' in *Between Demonstration and Imagination: Essays in the History of Science and Philosophy Presented to John D. North*, edited by Lodi Nauta and Arjo Vanderjagt (Leiden: Brill, 1999), page 126.

[63] *Ibid.*, page 127.

[64] *Ibid.*, page 129.

[65] See Ioannis Marathakis, *The Magical Treatise of Solomon, or Hygromanteia* [SOURCE-WORKS OF CEREMONIAL MAGIC, Volume 8] (Singapore: Golden Hoard Press, 2011), "the Greek original of the *Key of Solomon* for the first time in English." A partial English translation of the *Hygromanteia* appears as APPENDIX 1 of Pablo A. Torijano's *Solomon the Esoteric King: From King to Magus, Development of a Tradition* (Leiden: Brill, 2002).

Genealogiæ or *Fabulæ* (probably 2nd century AD), where "the hours were the daughters of Jove and Themis."[66]

Following this tradition, many books of magic contain sections detailing the operations and spirits of the hours of the day and night. Where many of these works give planetary rulers, names, ruling angels or spirits, virtues, etc., for a cycle of twenty-four hours for each day of the week, our MS of *Liber Lunæ* gives but one cycle for "whatever day thou wilt."

Works which contain accounts of the hours of the day and night include

- The *Heptameron,* or *Magical Elements,* attributed to the thirteenth-century magician Peter de Abano and usually appended to the pseudo-Agrippan *Fourth Book of Occult Philosophy,* lists the names of the hours of the day and night early in the text. Toward the end of the work, after outlining 'Considerations' for each of the days in turn, the *Heptameron* includes "Tables of the Angels of the Hours according to the course of the dayes," which shows the rotation of hourly angels through all seven days in a manner similar to the *Hygromanteia*; indeed, the head angels in the *Heptameron* match those of the *Hygromanteia* for Sunday, Monday, and Tuesday, thereafter showing Raphael, Sachiel, Anael, and Cassiel.[67]

- S. L. MacGregor Mathers' edition of *The Key of Solomon* shows a "Table of the Magical Names of the Hours, and of the Angels who rule them...." The magical names of the hours match those in the *Heptameron,* but the angel names, though the same and in like order, are displaced by twelve hours, the rotations commencing at noon rather than midnight. The *Key*'s BOOK I, CHAPTER II briefly reports "Of the days, and hours, and of the virtues of the planets," following the notion and order as *Hygromanteia,* but referring to the Hebrew names of the planets (*Shabbathai, Tzedek, Madim,* etc.) rather than the Greek gods associated with them.[68]

- *The Pauline Art,* the third book within the seventeenth-century composite *Lemegeton* or *Lesser Key of Solomon,* gives the names, angelic rulers, dukes, servants, and seals of the hours of the day and night "for any day." While the *Pauline Art* introduces each hour – except the first – with its name ("The second

---

[66] page 130.

[67] See *The Fourth Book of Occult Philosophy,* edited by Stephen Skinner (London: Askin Publishers, 1978; REPRINT. Berwick: Ibis Press, 2005), pages 61 and 93-96, or *The Fourth Book of Occult Philosophy,* edited by Donald Tyson (Woodbury: Llewellyn Publications, 2009), pages 192 and 214-217. The *Heptameron* is the source of the lists of names and angels for the hours in Francis Barrett's *Magus*; see BOOK II, PART III, page 107: "A TABLE *shewing the* MAGICAL NAMES *of the* HOURS, *both* DAY *and* NIGHT," and BOOK II, PART IV, page 139: "...the Table of the names of Spirits and Planets governing the Hours."

[68] Refer to *The Key of Solomon,* edited by S. Liddell MacGregor Mathers (London: Redway, 1909; reprint. New York: Samuel Weiser, Inc., 1974; reprinted frequently), pages 8 and 11-14.

hour of the day is called Cevorym," "The 3rd hour of any day is called Dansor," etc.[69]) in a manner similar to *Liber Lunæ*, however, between the two works only a few of the names correlate: the ninth hour of the day, perhaps ('Baton' or 'Luron' in *Liber Lunæ* and 'Karron' in *The Pauline Art*, noted below) and the tenth and eleventh hours of the night, which are identical.[70] Beyond that, *The Pauline Art* gives account of the angels, dukes, and seals of the hours, whereas *Liber Lunæ* emphasizes the images and virtues.

Some works are closer to our *Liber Lunæ* in their general form and content than those just described. One text which is directly related is, of course, *Sepher ha-Levanah* (edited by Greenup), which includes sections on the names of the hours of the day and night and their images.

Another closely related text is the less familiar *Munich Handbook*, or *Munich Manual of Demonic Magic*,[71] a fifteenth-century manuscript described by Richard Kieckhefer, which gives an account of the names, angels, and "functions of images," which Kieckhefer conveniently presents in table form, in *Forbidden Rites: A Necromancer's Manual of the Fifteenth Century*.[72]

The functions, or virtues, of the hours given in *Liber Lunæ* generally match those in the *Munich Handbook*, whereas the names of the hours only occasionally suggest any correlation. The most similar are these:

- second hour of the day: *Liber Lunæ* – Yenor   *Munich Handbook* – Yan, Or
- ninth hour of the day: *Liber Lunæ* – Baton or luron *Munich Handbook* – Karon

The names of the hours in the *Munich Handbook*, the *Key of Solomon*, and *Heptameron* show great similarities, even with their variations of spelling and order. However, the names of the hours in the *Pauline Art* are rarely similar to those in any of these other magic texts. Note, however, the ninth hour of the day of the *Munich Handbook* and the *Pauline Art*, which give 'Karon' and 'Karron,' respectively, and the twelfth hour of the day where *Heptameron* and *Pauline* Art give 'Natalon' and 'Nahalon,' respectively.

More interesting in the present context is that the *Pauline Art's* 'Nahalon' for the 12th hour of the day is somewhat similar to *Liber Lunæ's* 'Rabalon,' and the eleventh and twelfth hours of the night in the two texts are identical: 'Mal(c)ho' and 'Aalacho.'

---

[69] Peterson's edition, pages 112-113.
[70] Refer to Joseph H. Peterson's edition, *The Lesser Key of Solomon* (York Beach: Weiser Books, 2001), pages 110-129, or *The Goetia of Dr Rudd*, edited by Stephen Skinner and David Rankine (London – Singapore: Golden Hoard Press, 2007), pages 311-323.
[71] Bavarian State Library Codex Latinus Monacensis 849.
[72] Tables F and G, pages 182-183. University Park: Pennsylvania State University Press, 1997.

These and other comparisons can be made using *Table 4*, below.

Elsewhere within Sloane MS 3826 there is material which supplements *Liber Lunæ*'s HOURS, i.e., *fols.* 65-67v and *fols.* 78-80, which are parts of the ranging mid-section of the manuscript (*fols.* 57-83v). A transcription of these passages appears below within § SUPPLEMENTARY MATERIAL.

Table 2

HOURS OF THE DAY[73]

HOUR	NAME	FUNCTION
1	*Vebiche*	hiding
2	*Yenor*	love, profit
3	(no name given)[74]	fowls, fish
4	*Oelghil*	reptiles, scorpions
5	*Coaleth*	wolves, foxes, cats
6	*Jehunoᵉ conchor*	captives
7	*Jador*	entering to kings
8	*Jasolun,* or *Jasumech*	confusion, desperation
9	*Baton* or *Luron*	binding thieves
10	*Sachon* or *Sahon*	loosening the mouths of kings
11	*Jebrim*	good relations
12	*Rabalon* or *Vahialon*	binding tongues

---

[73] *Liber Lunæ, fols.* 87-89v.
[74] Sloane MS 3826 *fol.* 78 gives the name of the third hour as *Ansur*.

Liber Lunæ

Table 3

HOURS OF THE NIGHT[75]

HOUR	NAME	FUNCTION
1	*Cefratetyn* or *Hamon*	baths, fires, silence
2	*Debzul* or *Canbeul*	preventing fornication
3	*Thaor*	getting rid of beasts
4	*Hallahay*	destroying
5	*Camfar*	calling forth storms, causing discord
6	*Zoran*	putting men out of their houses
7	*Jafor*	setting plants afire
8	*Myach*	gathering fowls
9	*Oritefor*	gathering fowls
10	*Malho*	causing the arrogant to depart
11	*Aalacho*	enticing another region
12	*Fellen*	tormenting

---

[75] *Liber Lunæ, fols.* 90-92v.

Table 4

NAMES OF THE HOURS OF THE DAY FROM FIVE SOURCES

Hours of The Day	LIBER LUNÆ	SEPHER HA-LEVANAH	MUNICH HANDBOOK [76]	THE HEPTAMERON [77]	PAULINE ART [78]
1	Vebiche	Yubitum, or Yebean	Yayn	Yayn	-
2	Yenor	Geornorim, or Genorim	Yan, Or	Janor	Cevorym
3	-	Banur, or Rampur	Nassura	Nasnia	Dansor
4	Oelghil	Tzelbim, or Tzel Gehem	Sala	Salla	Elechym
5	Coaleth	Tzealekh, or Tzlalekh	Sadadat	Sadedali	Fealech
6	Jehuno⁰ conchor	Tzidamor, or Tehmor	Tamhut	Thamur	Genapherim
7	Jador	Yador	Caror	Ourer	Hamarym
8	Jasonun, or Jasumech	Yaporim, or Yapoim	Tariel	Tanic	Jafanym
9	Baton, or Luron	Ra, or Baron	Karon	Neron	Karron
10	Sachon or Sahon	Yahim, or Yakhon	Hyon	Jayon	Lamarhon
11	Jebrim	Yebrim, or Yehrim	Nathalon	Abay	Maneloym
12	Rabalon, or Vahialon	Rayalom, or Rayalon	Abat	Natalon	Nahalon

[76] From Richard Kieckhefer's *Forbidden Rites*, pages 182-183.
[77] From Stephen Skinner's edition of *The Fourth Book of Occult Philosophy*, page 93.
[78] From Joseph H. Peterson's edition of *The Lesser Key of Solomon*, pages 112-129.

Table 5

NAMES OF THE HOURS OF THE NIGHT FROM FIVE SOURCES

Hours of The Night	LIBER LUNÆ	SEPHER HA-LEVANAH	MUNICH HANDBOOK [79]	THE HEPTAMERON [80]	PAULINE ART [81]
1	Cefratetyn, or Hamon	Amen, or Hanem	Leron	Beron	Omalharien
2	Debzul, or Canbuel	Thmbeyi, or Tibezimer	Latol	Barol	Panezur
3	Thaor	Thathor, or Dahor	Hami	Thanu	Quabrion
4	Hallahay	Alahir	Atyn	Athir	Ramersy
5	Camfar	Kamaypur	Caron	Mathon	Sanayfar
6	Zoran	Razom, or Zarori	Zaia	Rana	Thaazaron
7	Jafor	Yapor, or Yaper	Nectius	Netos	Venaydor
8	Myach	Zimali	Tafat	Tafrac	Xymalim
9	Oritefor	Tzepar, or Zeparim	Conassuor	Sassur	Zeschar
10	Malho	Nahalqo. Or Malko	Algo	Aglo	Malcho
11	Aalacho	Alako, or Alatho	Caltrua	Calerna	Aalacho
12	Fellen	Selem, or Shellem	Salaij	Salam	Xephanææ

---

[79] From Richard Kieckhefer's *Forbidden Rites*, pages 182-183.
[80] From Stephen Skinner's edition of *The Fourth Book of Occult Philosophy*, page 93.
[81] From Joseph H. Peterson's edition of *The Lesser Key of Solomon*, pages 112-129.

§ 4. THE FIGURES OF THE PLANETS

The section on THE FIGURES OF THE PLANETS breaks from the usual content of manuscripts bearing the title *Liber Lunæ*, which refers specifically to THE MANSIONS OF THE MOON and the images and virtues associated with them. Often appended to accounts of the mansions are treatments of the cycle of THE HOURS OF THE DAY AND NIGHT, as in our *Liber Lunæ* and Greenup's *Sepher ha-Levanah*.[82] However, the inclusion of THE FIGURES OF THE PLANETS, namely, the magic squares, their virtues and operations, under the title *Liber Lunæ* may be unique to Sloane MS 3826.[83]

In *Unlocked Books*, Benedek Láng writes.[84]

> The history of magic squares can be traced back to India and China, and a number of cases can be mentioned from the Islamic and Byzantine worlds until they made their famous appearance in the works of such Renaissance magicians as Cornelius Agrippa and Girolamo Cardano, not to mention the well-known square of four turning up in Dürer's engraving *Melancholia I*.

Liber Lunæ fols. 93r-96v closely resembles *De septem quadraturis planetarum* [ON THE SEVEN SQUARES OF THE PLANETS][85] which is discussed throughout Láng's *Unlocked Books*; a page from this manuscript is shown in Láng.[86]

This fourth section of *Liber Lunæ* is also similar to §§ 28-33 of the fifteenth-century *Liber de angelis, annulis, karecteribus & ymaginibus planetatium* (attributed to Osbern Bokenham, transcribed and translated by Juris G. Lidaka),[87] namely, *fols.* 134b-9 of Cambridge University Library MS. Dd. Xi.45. The number patterns in *Liber de angelis* for the figures of Saturn, Jupiter, Sol (if reversed), Venus (if reversed), and the Moon match those of *Liber Lunæ*. The number patterns for the figures of Mars and Mercury are, however, different.

---

[82] THE HOURS OF THE DAY AND NIGHT is frequently found as an independent treatise, as, for example, *Liber de imaginibus et horis* of Hermes and *Liber de imaginibus diei et noctis* of Belenus.

[83] *Liber Lunæ* and *De imaginibus septem planetarum* appear together—thought not under the same title—in other MSS, *e.g.*, Biblioteca Nazionale Centrale di Firenze (Florence) II-iii-214.

[84] Ibid, Page 91.

[85] Kraków, BJ 793, *fol.* 60r, fifteenth century.

[86] Page 84, Fig. 5. Láng notes the similarity of *De septem quadratris* and "the description of the planetary squares [which] follows *Liber Lunae*" in Sloane MS 3826 in *Unlocked Books*, page 91, note 21, referring to my 2003 edition at www.esoteric.msu.edu/Liber/LiberLunae.html.

[87] In *Conjuring Spirits*, pages 64-75.

As noted in the Láng citation, Agrippa includes a summary, "Of the tables of the planets [i.e., magic squares, called by Agrippa 'kameas'], their virtues, forms, and what divine names, intelligences, and spirits are set over them," as CHAPTER XXII of *The Second Book of Occult Philosophy*.[88]

Although some of the number schemes are reversed or rotated, Agrippa's squares for Saturn, Jupiter, Sol (if *Liber Lunæ* is corrected), Venus, and Luna (an exact match if *Liber Lunæ* is corrected) resemble those of *Liber Lunæ*. Agrippa's figures of Mars and Mercury show different number arrangements from those in *Liber Lunæ*. Note, however, that Agrippa's number patterns in the figures of Mars and Mercury match those in *Liber de angelis*.

British Library Harley MS 6482 treats the magic squares in § "Of the Little Tables of the Planets and of What Divine Names, Intelligences and Demons Belong to these Tables."[89] These were copied from Agrippa's *Second Book* by Dr Rudd (who is mentioned above) in the late seventeenth century.

As for the indications and directions associated with the magic squares, great similarities exist among all of these texts.

---

[88] Refer to Donald Tyson's edition of *Three Books of Occult Philosophy*, pages 318-328, and his APPENDIX V, "Magic Squares," pages 733-751.
   See also Barrett's *Magus*, PART II, CHAPTER XXVIII, pages 142-147.
[89] *A Treatise on Angel Magic*, pages 107-12.

THE TEXT AND TRANSCRIPTION

Liber Lunæ in Sloane MS 3826 is in Early Modern English with remnants of Middle English dispersed throughout. In her introduction to *The Watkins Dictionary of Angels*[90], Julia Cresswell writes of Sloane MS 3826,

> I would suggest that although the manuscript may be sixteenth century, some of the language is rather old-fashioned for that date, except perhaps for an old person writing in the early sixteenth century. I would guess that the text is a reworking of an earlier one, pushing the origin of the material back into the Middle Ages.

The manuscript is written in large, fairly even sixteenth-century longhand. Alas, it is not always easy to read; there are numerous ambiguous letters and words.[91] (Images of example folio leaves are shown within the transcription.) Fortunately, the scribe took some pains to print the lists of angel names and magical terms (which in my transcription are shown in *italics*). Indeed, the clearly rendered corruptions of the names of the Mansions of the Moon and the hours of the day and night, along with the odd number configurations in the figures of Mars and Mercury may at some point help us trace the immediate source(s) for our *Liber Lunæ*.

The text of *Liber Lunæ* has been literally transcribed with no changes in spelling or word order. Using superscript and other typographical features, I have imitated the conventions of the scribe and the look of the manuscript. Some examples:

- wch for *which*
- wth for *with*
- p^{ar}ty for *party* (meaning *part*) and pap^{er} for *paper*, while subtle variations on the shorthand

SUPPLEMENTARY MATERIAL

In addition to the transcription, I have prepared paraphrases of *Liber Lunæ* §§ 3. THE HOURS OF THE DAY AND NIGHT and 4. THE FIGURES OF THE PLANETS in contemporary English. Errors in the original text have been amended, and the four planetary figures which contain mistakes in the Sloane MS (Sun, Venus, Mercury, and Luna) have been corrected.

§ 1. THE MANSIONS OF THE MOON from the Sloane MS *Liber Lunæ* has not been modernized in quite the same way because its presentation in our MS is inconsistent and fragmentary. Instead, I have crafted a useable text by blending the mansions sections of *Liber Lunæ* and *Sepher ha-Levanah*, using the former as the base text.

Three excerpts from other parts of Sloane MS 3826 which correlate to sections of *Liber Lunæ* have been added:

- Supplement to *Liber Lunæ* § 1. THE MANSIONS OF THE MOON:
  - Sloane MS 3826 *fols*. 80-82v, which gives indications and procedural details not found in *Liber Lunæ fols*. 84v-86v.
- Supplements to *Liber Lunæ* § 3. THE HOURS OF THE DAY AND NIGHT:
  - Sloane MS 3826 *fols*. 65-67v
  - Sloane MS 3826 *fols*. 78-80
  These passages augment the material in *Liber Lunæ fols*. 87-92v.

For clarity, paragraphs have been imposed on the successive horoscopes and hours in the supplements. Otherwise, these texts have been directly transcribed.[92]

---

[92] A full transcription of British Library Sloane MS 3826 *fols*. 57-83v has been added as an appendix to the present work. This portion of Sloane MS 3826 awaits more careful rendering and research. My brief introduction provides little more than speculation on the nature of the text and its possible sources.

Liber Lunæ

TRANSCRIPTION

[84]

Liber Lunæ

In noie dnj̃ pii misericordis soli Deo honor &t
In the name of the meeke God and mercifull, to
God alone honor and glory This is liber ☉ that
is the booke of worching that is said *Liber Lunæ*
the circle of wch is to the dwellers of the earth
It is sothely a booke knowen, and it is cleped as I
have said *Liber Lunæ* wherein be the privityes of old
wise men that were hid to all men. And he worcheth
wth it in all men that inhibiteth the earth, and in all
men that be under the circle of the moone that is
cleped the circle of this world he wrought wth it
fortune and infortune, profitt and impediment, good and
evill, and there belongeth unto yt xxviii mansions or
dwellings and xxviii worchings. None sothely of them
all is that is made or graven but when the moone
was in the same mansion diverse. It is the art of all
that fulfull not the worke or worching of the worcher
where it were good or evill.

Hermes said I have proved all the booke of all
planetts But I have not seene a truer neither a
p^erfecter then this p^arty most p^recious and they nempned
it *Librum Lunæ* And the first p^arty of *fallam^anah*[93] that
is before God I witnes and I admonish that thou hide
it from all men or els God will axe of thee what
ever were done by it in the day of Dome ffor wth it
may be done good things and evill in each moneth
and in eache day that thou wylt. And it is a most
p^recious booke and most secret ffor in it is the privy
name of God and unhable to be spoken wth wch he

---

[93] The word *fallam^anah* is a corruption of an Arabic phrase which means, as stated in the text, "before God I witness."

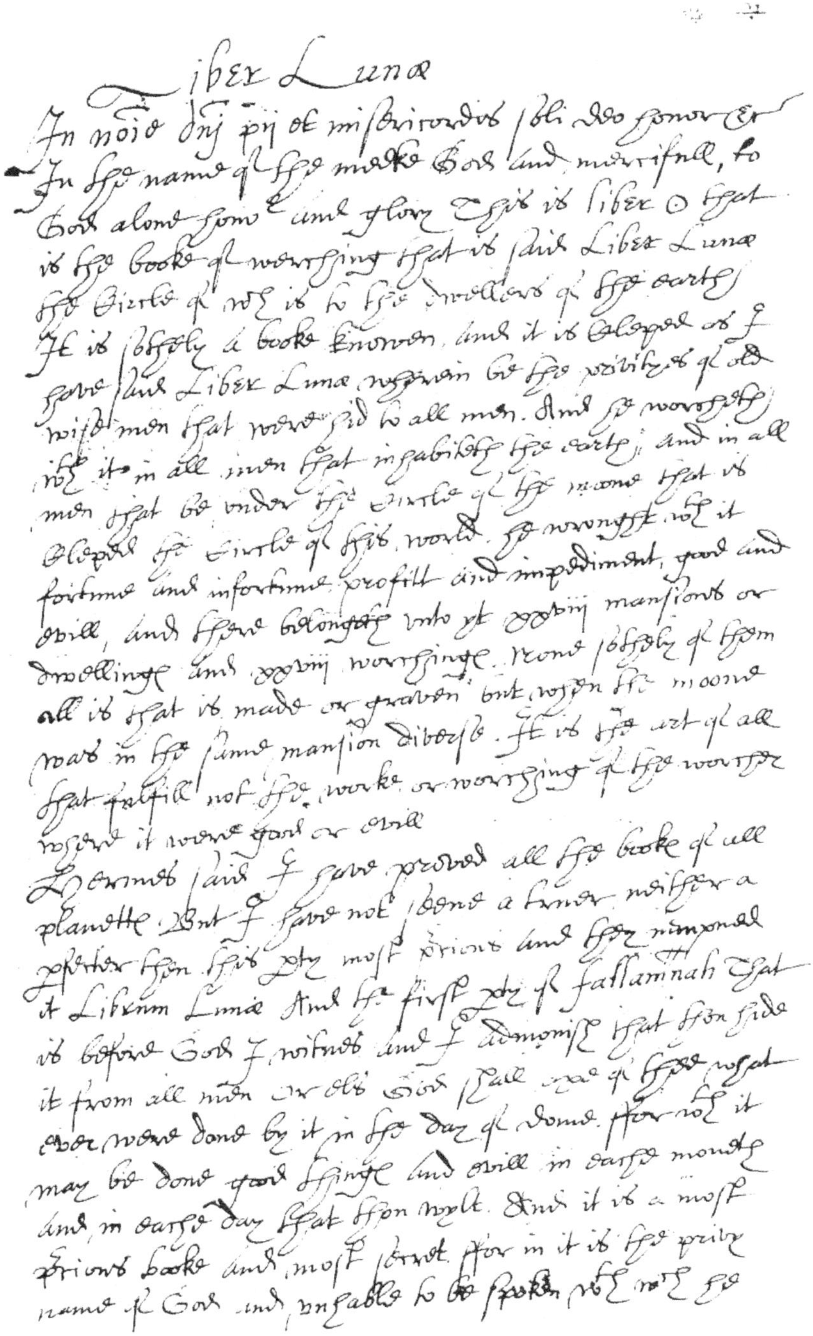

Figure 7: British Library Sloane MS 3826, *fol.* 84r: the first page of *Liber Lunæ*

[84v]

worcheth in all works good and evill ffor he
worcheth in it righteous and unrighteous & contrary
Keepe therfore that I have written to thee and
dread God and beware least thou shew it to
any man lest he lese men by it, neither touche he
it pollute, that is let him not do in it worchings
nor washings, and the worke will be magnified
and it is great. When thou hast made of it the
worching, thou shalt enclepe upon it the names
of angels serving to the circle of the moone.
suffume them 7 tymes wth precious aromaticks
and suffumiga^Cions And thou shalt make a cita^Cion
to it 7 tymes and thou shalt name these names
that thou wilt of wch thou hast made worching
and the name of the hower and the name of
Luna. and the name of the mansion in wch Luna
were, and the name of the day in wch he were
And if in the same mansions were sely and highe
under wch thou makest these most worchings were
effect. there will be speeding of the worke w^th
the helpe of God.

Bolemus said when *Meliatalh* that is Luna in
the first mansion that is the face of martis and
it is an evill mansion thou shalt make in it the
worching of Separation. *Albutaim* that is the
wombe of Ariets and it is fortuna az when
Luna descendeth in yt make ☉ of all things
to be bowed and of them whome thou wilt Joyne
togither.[94] *Aldeboran* 4th wch is the eye of Taurus
and it is the evill face of mercury. When Luna

---

[94] The third mansion is missing.

The account of the third mansion in *Sepher ha-Levanah* reads, "*Aqhoranay*, or *Alturayib* in another version, which means to say the end of Aries and the head of Taurus, and [the] white face. And *fortuna* [i.e., good fortune] from Venus. When the Moon was in it, the image of words of grace [are made], and the things you desired to join together should be made. And it is in the end of the second mansion and is limited to eight degrees within Taurus."

[85]

descendeth in it the worchings of all adversityes and
evills be made. *Almaycen* the 5 dwelling evill red
the face of Luna. When Luna descendeth in it the wor=
chings of all adversity and of alligaᶜion or building
there be made. *Althaya* the 6 mansion fortuna rubea
facies Saturni. When Luna descendeth in it the worch=
ing of them be they done wᶜʰ thou wilt fulfill the wor=
chings of God according and love be they made
Addiraen the 7 mansion and end of Geminory and is
interpʳᵉted *Brachia* and it is a fortune variant that is
white and red and the face of Jovis. When Luna descen=
deth in yt be there made worchings of all wylde
beasts of concord and of love and of all goods. *Innatar*
the 8 mansion and it is the head of Cancer fortuna
rubea and az the face of martis when Luna descen=
deth in it worchings of waters of shippes and of
flouds are they made. *Alkaud* the 9 mansion and the
wombe of Cancer and it is interpreted highnes, and
it is fortuna az or fortune or forme whyte then be
made the worchings of fowles as well of great as of
lesse and of culvers and thou shalt profitt. *Algeibh*
is the 10 man. It is thend of Cancer and the beginning
of Leo And it is interpreted the front of him and it is
fortuna az and the face of Venus wᵗʰ it make the
worchings of wolves of foxes and wylde beasts.
Azobra is the 11 mansion and the hart of Leo wᶜʰ by
another name is said *Azumble* wᶜʰ is evill blacke the
face of Mercury. When Luna descendeth in it be the
made the wirchings of sepᵃʳaᶜions and of alligaᶜions or
bynding of infyrmityes and distinction and thou shalt
profitt in them. *Algapha* is the 12 mansion and the
Cauda leonis and caput virginis for: alba. and the face

[85v]

of Luna. When he descendeth in it Do thou the
worchings of coniunction and of all things that
thou wilt shape. *Alans* is the 13 mansion and
the wombe of Virgo fortuna az the face of
saturne when Luna descendeth in it make workings of coniunction and of all things that thou
wilt shape and joyne togither. *Alchumech* is the
14 mansion thend of Virgo fortuna rubea a
starre profitable and good the face of Jovis when
Luna descendeth in it be there made worchings
of inclination and of all love and dilection
Algarst is the 15 mansion evill red the face
of martis and the head of Libra wch in it make
worchings of all evill and tribulation and destruction of hit whome thou wilt lett. *Azubene*
is the 16 mansion evill the face of Solis and
the middle of Libra wth it be there made the
works of sep^ara^Cion of Destruction and of all alliga=
tion and Impediment or letting. *Alichul* the
17 mansion and it is interpreted *Corona*. It is
sothely thend of Libra and the head of Scorpio
and it is evill the face of Venus. When Luna
descendeth in it make thy workings of good and of
tribulation and of all impediment. *Alcox* is the
18 mansion and the hart of Scorpio and it is
fortuna az the face of Mercury When Luna
descendeth in it make the workings of good and of
bynding of tongs and of all silence. *Alhebus* is
the 19 mansion that is to say *acus* that is a needle
It is sothely Scorpio Caudey and the head of Sagittary

[86]

fortuna az the face of Luna when Luna descendeth
in it make the worchings of fornication and of sedition
and of alligaᶜion and of luste. *Anahim* is the 20 mansion
and the wombe of Sagittary and it is the face of Saturne
When Luna descendeth in it make the worching of Inci=
sation of love and of concord *Alberda* is the 21 man=
sion and the end of Sagittary and it is fortuna alba
the face of ♃. When Luna descendeth in it make
the workings of Inclination. In it be made workings
of silence. *Ceadaebyh* is the 22 mansion and
the head of ♑ and it is evill fortune of desola=
tion after Aristotle cômixt the face of ♂ When
Luna descendeth in it make the workings of a good
hower and the faces of Luna according to love
and concord and reflexion the places of Luna to
discord and sepᵃraᶜion or Depᵃrting of all good
Azatalbuta is the 23 mansion an the hart of ♑
and the face of ☉ the fortune of him that swolow=
eth. When Luna descendeth in it that is in that
mansion then be made the works of all good
Zadac Zahond is the 24 mansion and it is Cauda
Capricorni and the head of ♒ And it is fortune
of fortunes the face of ♀ fortuna cú &c the wor=
chings of all good be they done. *Cealaghbrah*
is the 25 mansion of the wombe of ♒ and it
is the fortune of tents and the face of ☿ fortuna
az cú &c maketh the working of silence and bynde
under it what ever thou wilt. *Alfgarem* wᶜʰ is
the 26 mansion and the end of ♒ and the head
of ♓ the face of Luna. When Luna descendeth

[86v]

in it then be made the worchings of all recup^{era}=
tions and inclination and of dilection or love of
all things. *Alfgagir* is the 27 mansion and
the wombe of ♓ and evill mansion and red the
face of ♄ When Luna descendeth in it then be
made the workings of sep^{ara}^{C}ions or dep^{ar}ting and
of bynding and of all infirmityes. *Albecten* is
the 28 mansion and the cauda pisces and the face
of ♃ fortunate and when Luna descendeth in
it then be made the workings of all good and
of all profitt.

Suffumiga^{C}ions of worchings of dilection and of
reflexion and of all good these be the names
Alaod alkumeri - i - signu de Amnaria wch is some
Iland in the p^{ar}tyes of India *Azafran*.

Suffumiga^{C}ions of all dep^{ar}ting and of infirmity
and impediment thus be nempned *alnafac alas
ecfor aloes ni~gni azandall alagmars* of everich of
them the 4th p^{ar}t of an ownce And thou shalt
exercise in all the hower of suffumiga^{C}ion aswell
in the works of good as of evill by 55 angells of
whome these be the names *Comeil Cemeil
Charochin azardin reanei abras achithim abran=
casai larabusin Iangas mangarozan mamenim hacse=
mim mimgogm labelas mezetin farbarakin canda=
negin iaciz andonin rasaidin saphianim barthaylin
aninei Neilin borcolin balkanaritin arieisin abra=
norin cannamdin andalasin carnnamdin sarajemin
Adiamenim soe saeosin Jachehay feresin deibenim*

[87]

*mediesin heizamamin Janozothin Abramathin bifulica
begehalodin gaforin azafirin barionin matnairelin
genira manderilin.*

Bolemus said of these that be necessary this is the
liga^{C}ion or bynding, provide to all tongs & harts
of them that be accusors and of envious men into
worlds of worlds Make ☉ of him whome thou wilt
bynde and write in the forehead of him the name
of Luna that tyme and these names of angels
under ☉ wch is made be they written, whether it
be a signe orientall or occidentall meridionall or
septentrionall that is to say East or West North
or South wch names be these and the names of
their signes of the same p^{ar}ty write truely in the
ridge [rim] of ☉ name be wch God formed heaven and
earth sea and whatsoever is in them And also
write these names for to lett what ever thou wilt
lett by the worching of bynding and of prosperity
aswell of the sonnes of Adam as of other beasts
wilde fowles and fishes, and thou shalt grave each
p^{ar}ty of it And the angels, and if thou readest these
names to all thing that thou wilt read tho that be
used these sothely they be *Lahagenim lagha
laghoo layafurin uabalkanarithin. laiagelm. Laiasele=
syn.* But for these names be said to have double
effect, it is bound sothely to them what ever thou
wilt bynde or thou might let to the same to lose or
grant what ever thou wylt. But how these ought
to be done say we. When it is intended to this that

[87v]

The worching of ligaᶜion or bynding be made
say the names abovesaid as it is said before
in the hower of graving of the worching ffirst
they be red by order if the worke of expulsion
ought to be done, the names be they red thorder
before sett thus for the travaile will not meve
of him that intendeth these names sothely by night
from other hid but be he ware that when he
cometh to the ficle[95] of any worching in the
hower of graving of the names that he reade
name what ever he will as regions cityes
townes howses man and woman wilde beast
and other beast cloudes wyndes bird or fishes
or what ever he will bynde or lett after the
foresaid reason sothely read he and he will pʳᵒfitt
by the power of the creator. This bynding sothly
is proved and it is hid to the eyen mouthes harts
and tongs into words the name of the hower
Vebiche

The 2 worke is made in the 2 hower of what
ever day thou wilt, and it is said the worke of
love and reflexion and of profitt concord
Therefore be made twey worchings of tymes
wᵗʰ heads fused in the 2 hower and the names of
their lords in their heads be graven. In the brest
sothely the name if the Lord of the hower and
in the wombe these names following be they
written these sothely done, wᵗʰ good waxe be they
Joyned togither in the brests, afterward be they
buried in the house of thee and in the hower of
Sepulcher the 7 names of the first hower be they

---

[95] The word here is clear: *ficle*. I have not found any other examples of its use as a noun. In the present context, it seems to mean *instability* or *wavering*, like *fickleness*.

[88]

red by right order and they loveth themself ever
more. These be the names *Melkailin. Cadnaelin
Amonayelin. farcelin. uorayeylin. affayelin. Badray=
eylyn. Machiel. Canariel. Amymaryil. Fariel
noreil azareil Batraiel* The names of the hower
yenor.

The third worching is made in the 3 hower of
whatever day thou wilt, and it is sayd the worke
of all fowles or fishes and it is of bynding, and be it
of tyme of a man or woman or of this whome thou
wylt bynde. And the 7 precious names of the first
hower be they written in the wombe, the name of
the Lord in the head, and the name of the hower in
the brest, and suffume it wth cleane aloes and santalo
rubeo. and it be buried in the place of the same
thing of which the worke were for wonderfull things
should be seene of velocity or swiftness of obedience
of the same by the commandement of God. also
the names be then red of the first hower by order
of the name of the hower (answer)[96]

The 4th worching is made in the 4th hower of what
ever day thou wilt make the working of a serpent of
silver or of scorpions and Reptiles letting or of dragons
It is sothely the worching of divers wilde beats. Be
it made to the likenes of wch thou wilnest the binding
The name sothely of the same beast in the head. And
the name of the Lord of the hower in the brest. and
then the 7 names of the first hower in the wombe
be they written. And be it buried in the place of the
same thing for they will not remayne there. And in

---

[96] No name is given for the third hour, just the word *answer* in parentheses as shown. Sloane MS 3826, *fol.* 78r, gives *Ansur. Sepher ha-Levanah*, [Fol. 3a] has *Banur*, or *Rampur*.
See Supplementary Material: Supplements to *Liber Lunæ* § 3. the hours of the day and night.

[88v]

the hower of sepulcher or graving the 7 names
of the first hower be they red the name of the
hower turned *Oelghil*

The 5ᵗʰ worching is made in the 5 hower of
whatever day thou wilt and it is said the worching
of wolves of foxes of cats and of other such. The
worching be it made of silver to the likeness of
wᶜʰ thou wilt. and the name of this in the head
and of the hower in the brest, and the 7 names of
the first hower be they red. suffumigaᶜion of aloes
and indo turned. The name of the hower *Coaleth*.

The 6 worching is made in the 6 hower of what
ever day and it is said the over corner of captives
and of them that be prisoned, and of them that be
constrained and it is of bynding be it made of the 6
hower of tyme to the working of a man. the name
of the Lord in the head and the hower in the
brest, the 7 names of the first hower in the wombe
and beware that thou reade evermore the names of
the first hower doing and naming as he teacheth
in this suffumigaᶜion wᵗʰ aloes and sandalo rubeo
And betake it to the men for whome it is made for
from the destruction for wᶜʰ it were made seene he
will be delivered. Also do thou for eche neede or
noy from wᶜʰ thou wouldest be delivered the name
of the hower *Jehunoᵉ conchor*.

The 7 worching is made in the 7 hower of what
ever day after the strength and order wᵗʰ wᶜʰ
it is profitable to enter to kings that by it most
worship be gotten wᵗʰ dilection or love be it made
of silver best compowned upon the head of him the

[89]

name of the king in the brest the name of the lord of
the hower and the 7 names of the first hower or of the
second hower in the wombe be they written. This working
thus compowned be it borne at the entring before
kings the name of the hower *Jador*.

The 8 worching is made in the 8 hower of what ever
day and it is of confusion and disp^{era}^{C}ion least he may
dwell in houses or in habitacions make the working of
Saiac that is of an hound of red brasse wth twey heads of
wch one be of a man and thother of an hound and write
the name of the man upon the head of him, and the
name of the hower in the brest of him and the 7
names of the first hower in the wombe and suffume
wth the bloud of an hound slaine or wth the fatnes
of an hound thou shalt bury it at thy liking for thou
shalt see wonderfull things The name of the
hower *Jasolun* or *Jasumech*.

The 9 working is made in the 9 hower of what ever
day and it is said thop^{era}^{C}ion of bynding of theeves
make the op^{era}^{C}ion of a man of silver and the name of
this theefe in the head, and the name of the hower in
the brest, and the 7 names above, and the names of
angels of obstruction or stopping and suffume thou wth
aloes and croco and thou shalt bury it where thou
wilt and the theeves will be stopped leesing their
mindes or againe bearing and nothing stealing and de=
liverance of them is made The name of the hower
is *Baton* or *luron*

The 10th op^{era}^{C}ion is made in the 10 hower of what ever
day and it is for to lose the mouthes of kings or of riche
men or of diverse men. Be there made the op^{era}^{C}ion of a
man of silver and the name of angels of love and

[89v]

bynding and the name and the hower that is of the
second hower suffuming of ligno aloes indo zapharan
piloso and be it done as above. and beare he wth
him in a cleane white cloth of sylke the 7 names
in order be they red The name of the hower *Sachon*
or *Sahon*

The 11 hower and it is to dilection and reflexion
betwixt twey odiously having themself to be restored
be there made twey op^{era}C$^{}$ions of silver or of time
and the names of the lords in the head and in the
brest the names of dilection or love that is of the
second hower and as above suffumiga^{C}ion be it
made conveniently wth good odors wth aloes and
zapharan be it buried nigh an easy fier & faire
and they will come to thee and they shalbe ioyned
also the name of the hower *Jebrim*.

The 12 op^{era}C$^{}$ion is made in the 12 hower of what
ever day and it is to bynde tongs be there made
the op^{era}C$^{}$ion of tyme to the likenes of a man whome
thou wilt bynde the name of the Lord in the
head and the name of the hower in the brest
and as above the 7 names in the wombe and
suffumiga^{C}ion as above wth ligno aloes zapharan
thou shalt bury it in the house wth thee cleanely
and in white silke in the rigg name one i. normet
wth stoning wch be of 2 op^{era}C$^{}$ion of anentis philosopher
hide thou it under the constellation 7 nights reading
each night the names of the first hower be ther red
And suffume thou be 7 nights saying *Tu exumleazart
et sandalos* the name of the hower *Rabalon* or
vahialon

[90]

Dixit Bolemus dũ quæreret ab eo quidã &t
Bolemus said while Salomon sought of him that
he should ordeine a bath to them or a fier privily
The first hower of whatever night beginne thou the
worke of bathes or of fyers or of silence
Take scorp i. ferrus or yron and as fusu that is brasse
melte, make a candle that is to say a vessell having
4 or 6 mouthes[97] and upon every mouth thou shalt
grave these names severally *Secesyn hayfaysyn
harshin saluj seshin hershdiel remeahalyn Clodel
Isus mahede*. And in the neather p^{ar}t of the vessell
and in everich mouth be a pap^{er} made wett in oyle
and in the neather p^{ar}ty of the vessell these names hid
be they graven wch be of stonyng these as *Noryn
badichin. Anadyn. Sibir sanaphinin. halkars. ahadichin
anadyn. bahadin. Sanachin ranchbaili Jahudnil*. And
make upon the vessell the op^{era}^Cion of a man of brasse
having a brasen pottell powring out of oyle into the
vessell, and be there oyle in the vessell, that be
not wth the hand expressed and grave upon the
face of the worke these two names *chichud ephil*
The first name in the wombe and that other in the
neather p^{ar}ty of the vessell write *ib* И5 and tend
or kindle all of the pap^{er}s, and afterward close it
wth a covercle accordingly that it not be harmed
under this evermore. or make upon a vessell an
hollow bottom and the water will be hott for
evermore The name of the hower is *Cefratetyn*
or *Hamon*.

The second op^{era}^Cion is of abcision of fornication
and that is made in the second hower of everich

---

[97] *Sepher ha-Levanah* indicates that this "vessell having 4 or 6 mouthes" is instead a candelabrum or *menorah* with *seven* 'mouths' and that each "paper made wett in oyle" is a 'wick.'

[90v]

night. Bolemus said w^thin the city that is
cleped *Laumdarah* and ordeyne thou op^eraᶜion
in it That the woman do not fornication in it
w^thout end wch thus is made Take an op^eraᶜion
of cleane brasse and write in it these names
following *Myant. chelem. faroc. kahumcul
nohegemah* and these upon the face of the op^era=
tion *fecherah harsoleth iasad nadnad lecchat
badah.* And know thou that the first names
that is *Mynat* etc. ought not to be written in
the op^eraᶜion but in a brasen plate and put it in
the hand of th op^eraᶜion. And then thou shalt
bury the op^eraᶜion lest any man see there where
ever it were buried woman will not do for=
nication but region will cleave to Also thou
to fishes reptiles to water leches, and to frogs
and to all that letteth The name of the hower
is *Debzul* or *Canbeul.*

The third op^eraᶜion is made in the 3 hower of
everiche night and it is to put away beasts
as serpents scorpions attercoxs hounds mice
and other such when thop^eraᶜion were profitt
or made of tyme to the likenes of wch thou wilt
write in the face these names *Myatyon boroyon
fafraril.* And bury it when thou liketh and they
will not remayne or abide The name of the
hower is *Thaor* .

The 4th op^eraᶜion is made in the 4th hower of what
ever night and it is to destroy howses townes cityes
and divers tents or what ever thou wilt of thine

[91]

enemyes that is negation œste &c Take & anoynt
behind thop^{era}^Cion of a camyl i urna marin. and
write in the p^{ar}ty of it wth hit *afflaceros ffeygiltans*
ffeyglah ceidarophin And then say *Adinro vis vt*
sicut adurnit p^{ar}tes ligneæ in igne sic adurat regis
vel quicquid vis That is to say I adiure you that as
treen p^{ar}tes brenneth in the fyer so burne the
region of what ever thou wilt naming such the sonne
of such N moder and thou shalt name only what other
thing thou would then the names, and read the 7
names turned in the letters for this is the privity
of them The name of the hower is *Hallahay*.

The 5 op^{era}Cion is made in the 5 hower of what evr
night. and it is to destroy the hoast of cloudes of
haile and tempests, and for to cast among men
discord Be there made as above said 2 op^{era}Cions
of a double man of 4te of lead s.r pound and of
brasse 2to grave in it these names of angels
Nesahælmiel Jeszarailin. Jszunielaie. atfamin renormen
sekarkabel aragi mihan Jehabey bedyemyekalkel These
be the names of provocation of whome ever thou wilt
to thee I can sothely worche be them for great effect
will follow. Also *badakatir chen⁹ syelchech* And thou
shalt suffume it and bury it in an higher place
and if thou wilnest the destruction of a region or
another to be put away etc read the 7 names turned
The name of the hower is *Camfar*.

The 6 op^{era}Cion is made in the 6 hower of what ever
night and it is to put any man out of his howse lest
he dwell make the op^{era}Cion of a man of red brasse

[91v]

and write in it the names of expulsion and
suffume it, and write the name of it in the
head of him, and let it be in the house of him
for whome it is made, and he will go out fly=
ing to another region by 10 miles of for p^ertur=
ba^cion of his being and losing of his witt.
These be the names of expulsion *belychiechyn*
Raysel. abrail. aflin. cadeneul. miamem. bafreni
geraodin. barcaiol. analin. forachi. cafalin seche
other names for to bren wch is *Amagnis* &c.
And take thilke 7 names of the first hower and
be they red. the name of the hower is *Zoran*

The 7 op^era^cion is made in the 7 hower of what
ever night and it is to combustion of grapes
and sement of trees make a worke of red brasse
and grave in it these names ⊐⊏ ⋜ *; pope per*
combustione^s ⅄4 ᴔⱧ· *pir* ℔· ⅚ *byablib. gehil*
*combure d*⁹ *nissu et* rede the 7 names turned thou
shalt bury it in the terme of that place and
that region of them will brent by 10 mile
or after that thou wilt by bidding of God
wth heavenly fyer The name of the hower is
Jafor

The 8 op^era^cion is made in the 8 hower of what
ever night and it is to gather togither beame
fowles or collors in what ever maner thou wilt
make the ☉ to the similitude of wch thou wilt
of the best gold and put to the weight of mettall
and grave in it these names *Jerodah Carmetah*
adesach . achil . gabriel afferent vos ad me that

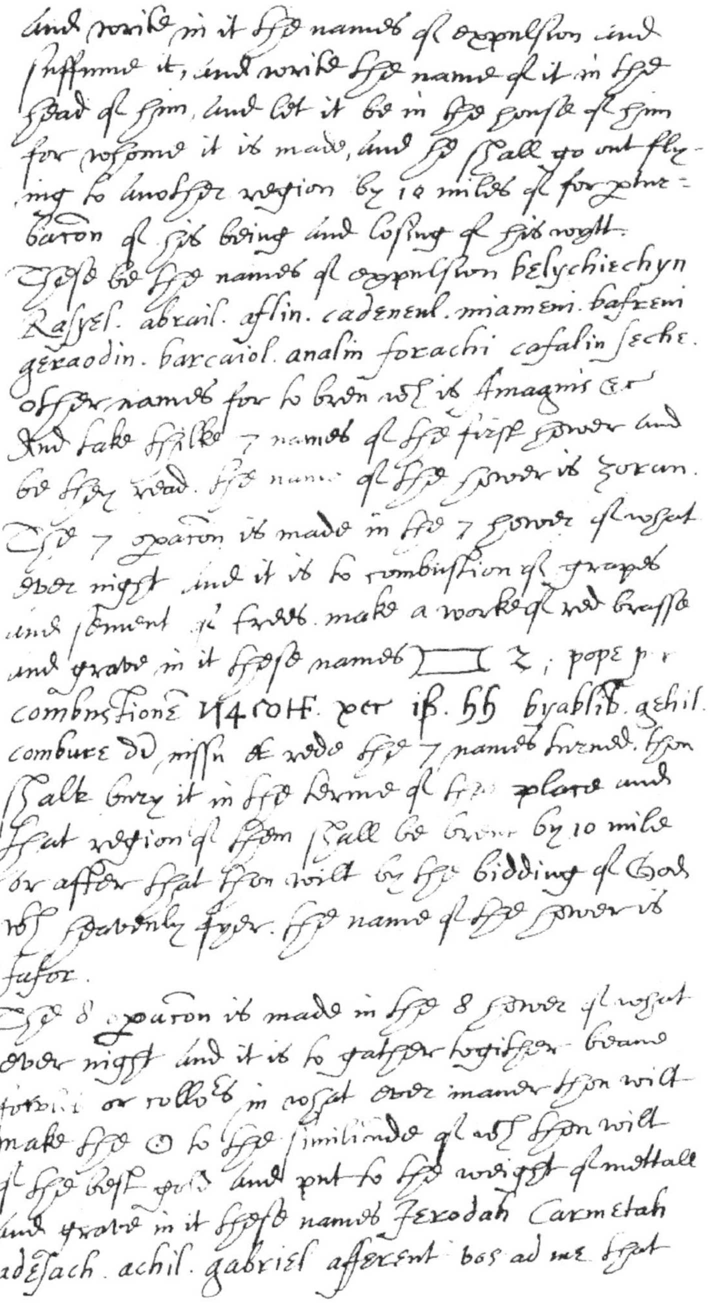

Figure 8: British Library Sloane MS 3826, *fol.* 91v – *Liber Lunæ*

[92]

is to say bring yoᵂ to me. Be it buried in the
higher place of the towne or of the night. Also of
other things wᶜʰ thou wilt gather togither the 7
names be they red by right order and this orison
is to be written *ápes in oi loco et parte adducat*
vos Gabriel de diversis plagis. Also do thou to eche
thing wᶜʰ thou wilt gather togither The name of
the hower *Myach.*

The 9 opᵉʳaᶜion is made in the 9 hower of what ever
night and it is as above to collection of fowles to
an hill wᶜʰ thou wilt make the ☉ to the likenes of
whay thou wilt of an ownce of gold followe and the
names of the angells in the next beforesaid in the wombe
be they graven and be it buried as above And the
7 names of the first hower be they red by order
The name of the hower *Oritefor.*

The 10 worching is made as abovesaid in the 10
hower that it is to depᵃrting of them that loveth them
self that they be not isyued neither be concurrent
wᵗʰout end make the opᵉʳaᶜion of tyme to the length
of a palme and the 4 pᵃrty be it made of red brasse and
be there sothely twey opᵉʳaᶜions and the head of one
be it the head of a shee beare and the head of that other
bee it of an hound, and the names of them be ther
graven in the heads and in the ridge [rim] of the 7 first
names and be it suffumed wᵗʰ stinking things And
be they buried in divers placs one in the east side
another in the west And to all things that thou
wilt depᵃrt these be the names *Gzorabi Izora*
hauli haule memoy nahualiemin matmoial

[92v]

kaihal malegen. moiogil. muctril muchil The
name of the hower *Malho.*

The xi[th] op[era][C]ion is made in the 11 hower of
what ever night and it is when thou wilt intice
or take away of another region to thee, make this
op[era][C]ion as fayre as thou might of silver or tyme
and grave his prop[er] name in the head and these
in the wombe *aragi rahian bedien Jahekalkel*
agnis kannaizozo maron kamerache emtelh amo=
koydar rasdar monras kaydich hartah. This orison
sothely wth these names in the operation be it written.
Ignis de cælo combur per comburente ☉ com
bureus bihu el alhalil combur jussu dei The
name of the hower *Aalacho.*

The 12 op[era][C]ion is made in the 12 hower of what
ever night and it is to torment much and to quaking
of the body wch thou wilt make thop[era][C]ion of a man
of red brasse of wch the necke be it large and
the face toward the ridge [rim] and the feet in steed
of the hands and againward And the name of
the Lord in the and of the planet in the
brest and the names of stoning in the ridge [rim] *aeol*
alkeguh hun aguh maeraszach sagellesz mausz
mahuh tortolaac Iblin Be it buried at the gates
of him. the name of the hower *fellen.*

Adhuc sequnt[r] 4 operaciones max[&] diei &c
yet followeth 4 op[era][C]ions most of the day or of
the night. The first op[era][C]ion is to lese whome thou
wilt And of losing of wylt or of lyfe. Be it made

[93]

of red brasse and the name of the Lord in the head
and in the ridge [rim] these names before written thou shalt
grave and he will be made sicke and he will be
troubled, and thou shalt bury it in the place of a dead
man unknown
The second op^{era}Cion is to remove from a towne where
thou wilt make the op^{era}Cion of *Subalfrage* most newe
of 6 expound The middle of wch be it of lead and thother
p^{art} be it of red brass. And grave in it these names
undatos haibiros kalome And 9 dnē *carnee armeche*
serath makamil. Inaceleme celub. And make 2 op^{era}Cions
follow of them. Be one in the ridge [rim] and the other in the
wombe Afterward suffume it wth the fatnes of an hounde
and thou shalt reade upon it 7 names of the first hower
turned And thou shalt bury it in the place of the east
of the castle for they will not remayne there one
day or night.

Now followeth the figures of
the Planets

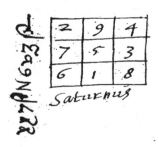

The figure of Saturnis is quadrate
and there be in each side of the
figure 3. When thou wilt worche
by this figure Saturnis be he
direct increasing the moone In the
day of Saturne and in the first hower
of it made or yt is better in new cotton and bynde
it to the thigh of a woman traveling in childe
bearing and anon wthout p^{er}ill she will be delivered
of the childe bearing And if thou suffumest thilk figure

[93v]

wᵗʰ thure and beareth it wᵗʰ thee thou shalt not
dread a king neither any other pᵉʳson willing to
annoy thee. And thou shalt have of them that
thou covetest reasonably. And if thou writest this
figure in lead Saturne being retrograde or again
ward going or diminute to light or under the beames
of stationary, and puttest it in a new building or in a
new plantation it will never be filled or stored wᵗʰ
people but men will fly from it. And if thou puttest
it in the seat of a pʳᵉlacy some he will be disposed
from it. I bid neverthelesse but that the charact
be written first above the figure.

The figure of Jovis is quadrate and
it is multiplyed by 4 etc in eche side be 34

When Jupiter were di=
rect make this figure in a
plate of silver in the day
of Jovis and in the hower
of him. And thou shalt suffume
it wᵗʰ ligno aloes and amber
and beare it wᵗʰ thee And
as many as seeme thee will

16	3	2	13
5	10	11	8
9	6	7	12
4	15	14	1

Jovis figura

be in love wᵗʰ thee and obey to thee. And if thou puttest
it betwixt the feet of a merchant his merchandise
will be increased. And if in a culver house or in the
place of bees they will be gathered togither. And who
ever being infortunate beareth it about him he will
be made fortunate from good into better soone.
And if thou puttest it in the seat of any prelate he
will dure raigne and prosper against all his ene=
myes and they may not do any annoy to him neither

[94]

he will dread them fforget not but to make the
characts above the figure

The figure of Mars
is quadrate or fowre
cornered & multiplied
by five, and there be in
eache side 65. It signi=
fieth warre and de=
struction. When Mars
were retrograde com=
bust diminute of light or number thou shalt grave
the figure of it in the day and hower of it in a plate
of copper and thou shalt suffume it wth menstruate
bloud, or wth the cloth of one that is hanged, or wth
the sword of one that is slayne or wth stercore murin
that is mice dirt or of catte. And putt it in a new house
or in a building and it will not be fulfilled but it
will be left wildernes. And if it be putt in the seat of
any prelate he will be made worse soone. And if in the
place of a marchant it will be destroyed all. And if
thou makest this in the name of 2 men loving them=
selves together hate will fall betwixt them and en=
mity if thou bury it in the house of that other of them.
And if thou doeth it while mars were direct or in=
creasing in number or light and suffume it wth red sylke
and saffron and wrappe it in the same silke and putt
it wth do thure or that is better cornelius wth
there that great lorde noy thee not neither domes men
neither enemyes, neither dome thine adversaryes and
also in battaile they will fly from thy face and they

14	10	1	22	18
20	11	7	3	24
21	17	13	9	5
2	23	19	15	6
8	4	25	16	12

Martis 69

[94v]

will dread, and they will be ashamed. And if
thou putt it upon the thigh of a woman she will
have menstrua. and if in virgin parchment. And
if thou putteth it in the place of bees they will fly
Also grave the characts above the figure.

The figure of Sol
is quadrate and there
be 6 multiplied by 6
and there be in eche
side 111. And it is to
kings and princes of
this world. And it is of
all lordship & power

1	32	34	3	35	6
30	8	27	28	11	7
10	24	15	16	13	23
19	17	21	22	18	24
10	26	12	9	29	25
31	4	2	33	5	26

figura Solis

when Sol wer in his exaltation in the 5th degree
of Aries. Take 6 3 [drams] of pure gold and make a round
plate and thou shalt grave on it the figure of Sol
in the day and hower of it and thou shalt suffume
it in muske and camfyre and thou shalt wash
 it in rosewater muske and camfer and wrappe it
in a cloth of yelow sylke And thou shalt hold it wth
thee. And thou shalt lead to effect whatever
thou wylt. And thou shalt get of riche men that
thou wilt. that thou be honoured among kings and
great lords and whatever thou shalt axe thou shalt have.

And whatever thou
seest for certaine shalbe
allowed to thee for good.
The figure of Venus
is quadrate And there
be 7 multiplied by 7
and there be in eache
side 175 and it is of

4	35	10	41	16	47	22
29	11	41	17	48	23	8
12	36	18	49	24	6	30
37	18	43	25	7	31	13
20	44	26	1	32	14	38
45	27	2	33	8	39	21
28	3	34	9	40	15	46

figura veneris

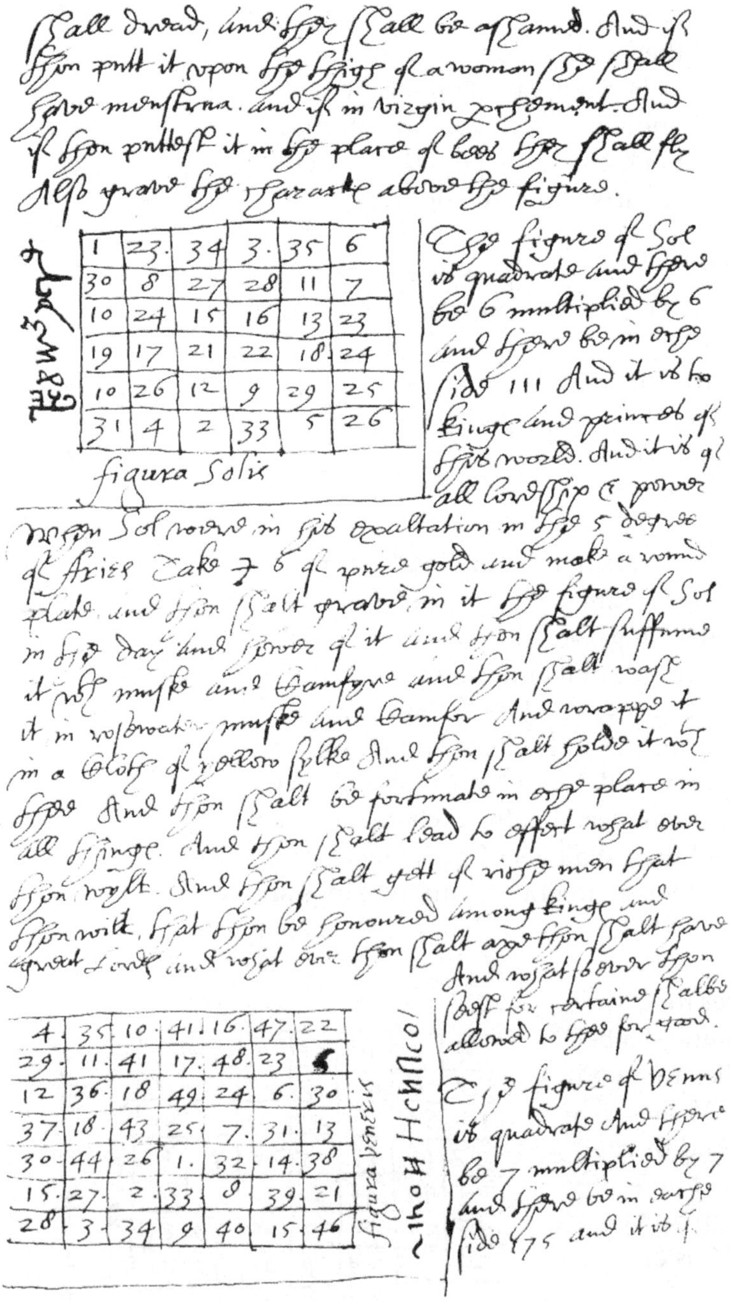

shall dread, and ther shall be ashamed. And if
thou putt it upon the thygh of a woman she shall
have menstrua. and if in virgin ... And
if thou puttest it in the place of ... ther shall ...
les grave the ... above the figure.

1	23	34	3	35	6
30	8	27	28	11	7
10	24	15	16	13	23
19	17	21	22	18	24
10	26	12	9	29	25
31	4	2	33	5	26

figura Solis

The figure of Sol
is quadrate and ther
be 6 multiplied by 6
and ther be in one
side 111 And it is the
kinge and prince of
the world. And it is of
all lordship & power

when Sol were in his exaltation in the 5 degree
of Aries take 7 ℥ of pure gold and make a round
plate. and then shalt grave in it the figure of Sol
in his day and houre of it and then shalt suffume
it with muske and camfore and then shalt wash
it in rosewater muske and camfor And wrappe it
in a cloth of yellow silke And then shalt holde it in
ther And then shalt be fortunate in one place in
all thinge. And then shalt lead to effort what ever
thou wolt. And then shalt gett of ryche men that
thou wilt, that thou be honoured among kinge and
great lords and what ever thou shalt ... thou shalt have
And what so ever thou
... for certaine shalt
... allowed to the for good.

4	35	10	41	16	47	22
29	11	41	17	48	23	5
12	36	18	49	24	6	30
37	18	43	25	7	31	13
30	44	26	1	32	14	38
15	27	2	33	8	39	21
28	3	34	9	40	15	46

figura Veneris

The figure of Venus
is quadrate And ther
be 7 multiplied by 7
and ther be in earth
side 175 and it is ...

Figure 9: British Library Sloane MS 3826, *fol.* 94v – *Liber Lunæ* showing the kameas in the text.

[95]
fortune prop^{er}ly in the face of women and in all love and
fairenes. And Venus be it in piscibus wch is the exaltacion
of it or in tauro or libra wch be the houses of it, and that
it be fortunate that is swifte in course increased of light
direct or even Take 7 3 [drams] of pure silver and make a plate
in the day and hower of Venus, and suffume it
wth ligno aloes amber and masticke, and put it in a white
cloth of sylke. And thou shalt see marveiles And if a man
or a woman tary to be wedded beare he hit wth him
and soone be shalbe spowsed. And if any man hate thee
wash it wth rainwater or of a well or of rosewater, and
give it to the hater to drinke and he will love thee
And thou shalt do that thou seethest. And if thou seethest
camomill and washest the figure wth that water and if
thou sprinkle the same in a place where is discord or
dread of Dome, all evill will cease and will be neigh and
wisedome. And if thou sprinkle that water where beasts or
merchandise be they will be multiplied and increased
And if thou puttest it in thy bed thou shalt about in coitu
and thou shalt be loved of her.

The figure of mer=
cury is quadrate
and there be 8
multplied by 8
and there be in
eche side 260 in
length and bredth
and overthwart
And mercury is
full swift in mea=

figura Mercurij

8	7	59	60	61	62	2	1
49	15	54	12	53	51	10	16
41	42	22	21	20	19	47	48
32	34	35	29	28	27	39	36
40	26	27	37	36	30	31	33
17	18	46	45	44	43	23	24
9	55	14	52	13	22	50	45
64	63	3	4	5	6	58	57

ving and inchanting of bowing he hath p^{ar}ty & nature

[95v]

of other planetts and of signes complexions and
also to him be given strengthes of soule or lyfe wisdome
of philosophy fowre wayes and description when mer=
cury were direct swifte in course Take 8 3 [drams] zara=
cenores of pure silver in the day & hower of [Mercury],
and thou shalt grave in it the figure of mercury, and
suffume it wth ligno aloes, gariophylli and masticke
and holde it wth thee and all things that thou axest
thou shalt have. And if thou hast not silver make it
of citrine paper for it availeth as much. And if thou
putt it in a place of prelacy or in a chaire of a prelate
he will dure against his enemyes, and the gads
of the same will be increased And if thou makest
it in a ring in glasse or in a basen, or in a glasen
plate in the first hower of the day of [Mercury], in the
first 7 dayes of Lunation, and doest it away in the water
of a well and drinkest it be three dayes continuall
knowe thou that thou shalt leave all forgetfulnes
and thou shalt learne lightly that thou wilt And if
in steele of in a myrror and he that hath the palsy
beholdeth it, or he that hath spasmn they be cured
wth the sight alone. And also he that is blinded
for coitus will be cured And if thou fasteth by iii
dayes continuall onley to bread and hony and vuæ
passæ And afterward gravest it in citrine sylke
and suffumest it wth ligno aloes and sayest *O deus
per virtutes istius figuræ indica mitu in somnis i. quod
vis.* That is to say O God by the vertue of this
figure showe thou to me in sleepe that that thou wilt

[96]

and put under thy pillowe when thou lyest downe
write the characts first upon the figure

The figure of
Luna is quadrate
and there be 9
multiplied by 9
and there be in
each side 369
in lenth and
bredth and over=
thwart In the
day of Luna and
in the hower of

37	78	29	70	21	62	13	54	5
6	38	79	30	71	22	63	14	46
47	7	39	80	31	72	23	55	15
16	48	8	40	81	32	64	24	56
57	17	49	9	41	73	33	65	25
26	58	18	50	1	42	74	34	66
67	27	59	10	51	2	43	75	35
36	68	19	60	11	52	3	44	76
77	28	69	20	61	12	53	4	45

figura Lunæ

Luna increasing, in virgin p^{ar}chmt write it wth inke of
muske and saffron tempered wth rosewater, and suffume it
wth some cucumbis cucurbite and camfora and double the
scrowe and putt it in a plate of silver made to the maner
of a litle pipe or reeds and beare it wth thee. It availeth
also to axe all noble things and fulfilling, and that ta=
keth away all evill. And if thou dreadest an enemy in the
way, put it in the way, and thou shalt be delivered
from theeves and all evill. And thou shalt write in it
thincreasing of parchmt of a sheepe wth the bloud of a
black cocke that be gelded in the day of Luna in diminu^cion
In that of side sothely make thou the figure of Pisces
and Cancer wth thaforesaid bloud, and put that scrowe
in a litle pott full of water, and let it stande by a night
in the ayre. In the day following take the pott and say
go out N the sonne of N moder from such a place
or city that he be never returned to it held that water
in 4 p^{ar}tyes of the world. And that a woman never be

[96v]

wedded make it diminucion in the day and the hower
of hit in a plate of lead saying *Ligo* N *filia* N *vt*
nunqua~ nubat nec fructus faciat. That is to say I
bynde N the daughter of N that she never be wedded
neither make fruite and over that other side make
the ymage of the woman, and bury it in the sepulcher
of some man unknowen. And if you may not sell
thy merchandise write it in citrine pap[er] in the
increasing in the day and hower wth saffron tem=
pered wth rosewater and suffume it wth the first
suffumiga[C]ion and dowble the scrowe and put it w[th]
the things to be solde or to the necke of a beast
and they should be sold soone wth good delibera=
tion. *Deo gra[C]æ* thanked be God. These be
thaforesaid names *niselesayal nilegayal
Nihtiranaklaban nirufayal oohgal ahgal
ninegiohal.*

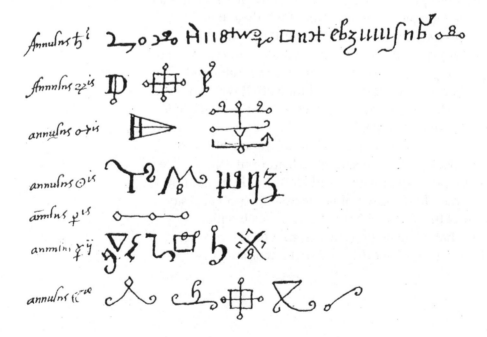

Figure 10: *Liber Lunæ* – ANNULI : *fol.* 96v.

[97]

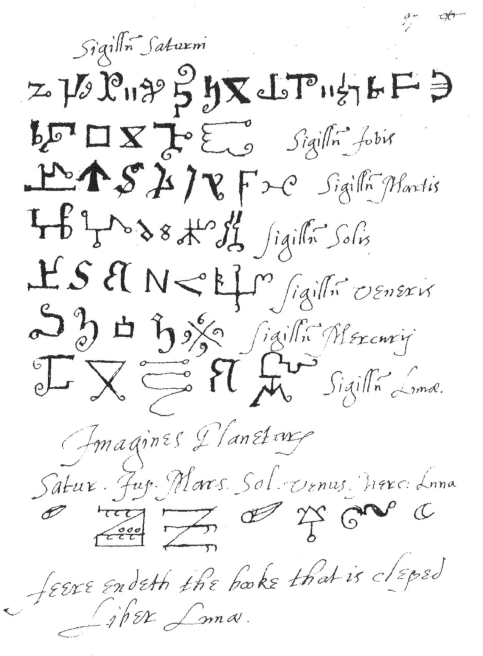

Figure 11: *Liber Lunæ* – SIGILLI : *fol. 97.*

ספר הלבנה.

THE

BOOK OF THE MOON

Edited, for the first time,

BY

A. W. GREENUP.

LONDON.

1912.

The MS. from which this work is printed is numbered
Or. 6360 in the British Museum collection. It is of
paper, $11\frac{7}{8} \times 7\frac{5}{8}$, and consists of 15 leaves. The
writing is Oriental Rabbinic of the 16th century. The
contents of the MS. are (1) fol. 1a—6b ספר הלבנה
(2) fol. 7a—11b ספר פעלות המזלות (3) fol. 12a—15b
A fragment of מפתח שלמה.

On the title page is the drawing of an astrologer,
compasses in hand, with one foot placed on the
Zodiacal sphere, within which are named the planets
and the earth. Above the head are eight stars, whilst
on the left hand top corner is a representation of
the moon and on the right of the sun. The MS. was
bought by the Museum Trustees from Raffallovich
and Lipkin in 1902, and, as far as the first two works
are concerned, is probably unique.

The contents of the ספר הלבנה may be summed
up thus :—

(1) Introduction in which the book is introduced
by some one under the name of הרמם. *
He says that all the books of astrology
which he is acquainted with are perplexing,
but that the one which commends itself to
him as the best and clearest is the
ספר הלבנה the first part of which follows.
It is not to be transmitted to any one and is
rightly considered a 'hidden' book.

* See Steinschneider, Heb. Uebersetzungen, p. 514.

(2) Twenty-eight directions for preparing צלמים in accordance with the various positions of the moon. As might be expected in a work of this kind there are many corruptions of Arabic names.

(3) Twelve directions as to the סמים to be used for good and evil צלמים.

(4) On the names of the hours of the night and their צלמים.

(5) Three short paragraphs headed פני המזלות. The first explaining that every מזל can be divided into three equal portions ; the second giving the signs of the zodiac ; and the third beginning פנים צומח.

(6) On the צלמים of the hours of the day.

In this last section occurs a mystical alphabet, evidently drawn from the Latin, and this would suggest that the whole work is a translation from some ancient Latin astrological treatise, "full of the most extraordinary medley of Greek, Babylonian, Egyptian, and other ancient traditions" (*Encycl. of Religion and Ethics*, iii. 454). The mystical alphabet occurs also in the ספר פעלות המזלות which may possibly be the second section of the ספר הלבנה referred to by הרמס in the preface.

ספר הלבנה.

אמר הרמם כתובי כל ספרי הכוכבים כולם
הנבוכים אולם לא מצאתי חלק יותר אמיתי ושלם
מהחלק המעולה הזה אשר קראוהו המשכילים
ספר הלבנה והוא החלק הראשון' ע"כ באדון
השמים אשביעך שלא תמסרהו לשום אחד כי אם
יצא ממנו דבר מעוקל הנה הבורא ית' מידך
ידרשנו' כאשר יכלול הפעל הטוב והרע בכל יום
וחדש אשר חפצת והוא ספר מופלג וחשוב וראוי
להעלם' ובו שם ה' הבלתי נקרא' ועל ידי זה
יעשה כל פעל אם טוב ואם רע' על כן את
האלקי' ירא והשמר מלמרות עיני כבודו ית''' ולא
תגלה הסוד הזה לוולתך' למען לא יצא ממנו רע
ואבדון' וכאשר חפצת לתקן איזה מהצלמים התרחק
מכל טומאה למען יושלם חפציך במעשיך.

הנה כאשר חפצת לעשות אחד הצלמים קרא
עליו שמות המלאכי' אשר למטה כעשנך אותו
כהעשנת משובחות ז"פ בהזכירך כל מה שחפצת
מאתו ושם השעה ושם הלבנה ג"כ שם העמידה'
ואם הי' בהמעמדות אשר תפעל בזמנם יהי'
כפרט הלבנה עם העזר האלהי וכו'.

אלו הם שמות המלאכים המשרתים ללבנה׃
ר"ל לצלמי הלבנה ולעגולו אשר בם תשביע על
כל צלם עם ההעשניות אשר למטה ז"פ בין
בפעולות הטוב או הרע׃ והם כ"ד מלאכים׃ אשר
סודותיהם הם אלו תטיב בהם ההבנה ושמרם
בשקידה מופלגת׃ אַנַאִילִים קוּנְצִילִים נַאשְׁגוּרָזִים
אַקאשִׁיַמֲדִי אֲמִיכִּילִים אַבְרַאכִיאָם אַבְרַאשִׁים
לַאִירַאיוֹזִים יַאמַאגהַאש מַאנְגָנִים מַאנְגוּרוּרַאם
הַארְטְנִינִי מוּנְטַאגִינִים לַאצַאנְדוֹנִים קַאמְשִׁילִינְדְרִים
שַׁאמַאם שַׁארַאִילִים אַמַאמִילִים הַקוּאִילִים
בַּאלְבַּנַארִיטָם אַרִיבַּיִּלִים בְּקִשְׁדָאִילִים אַבְּרַאנוּדוֹמִילִים
קַארְמַיִנָדִים אַנַדַאלַאשִׁים שַׁאַראהִיצִינִים אַדִיאַמֲנִים
צַאטַאהוֹטִים יַאצַארַרְפָנִישִׁים מֲאבְּינָאנִים נַהֲלִים
הִירַאמִינִים אַבְּרַאמַאטִים לַאנַאגוֹטִים׃ וְיפוּלַיַקַא
בְּלְֿגַאבַּאלְאִידִים גַאפּוֹרִים אַקְבַּאפָֿירִים טַאיִירִיאוֹמָֿם
דִיקוּמְיִילִים גְנִיטהוֹכִים מַאדַארִילִים כָּארְלְֿדִים
יְברוּנְכְֿלִים אַלַאדִים יַאבְּאלִים שֶׁאטְהַאכַּאם פַּאנַאפְֿלוֹר
בַּאבַּיְילִין דַאבְּנוּטִירוֹרִין.

אמר כאלינוס אפילו כאשר הלבנה באנאך
נ"א אלנאך אשר היא העמידה הראשונה ובמלואו
אמור סבובו והוא פנים ממאדים׃ תעשה צלמי
המחלוקת והשנאה.

א והעמיד ההוא תהיא הפנים הראשונים מטלה׃
ומתחיל מראש שלה׃ ויוגבל במעלה י"ב מטלה
וחצי מטלה והוא ראש שלה.

7

בֹּ אֵלבִּיזַאקָין נ"א אַלבָּוְקָאִים פורטונא לבנה פני
השמש ועמידה פורטונאטא (ר"ל הצלחה) כאשר
ירד אליה הירח ועשה בה התקוה וההשבה׳
וקניית האהבה והרֵעות׳ מַתחלת במעלה הי"ב
מטלה׳ וִיוגבל במעלה הכ"ו ממנו׳ והוא בטן
הטלה.

גֹּ אֵקהוֹרַבְנִ נ"א אַלטוֹרַאֵיָיב ר"ל סוף הטלה וראש
שור ופנים לבנים׳ ופורטונא מנוגה כאשר היתה
הלבנה בה יעשה צלם כל דברי חן והדברים
אשר חפצת לחברם׳ והיא בסוף העמידה השנֵיי׳
ומגביל במעלה ח' משור.

דֹּ אלדַּאבַארַם (אש .mg) היא עמידה אינפורטונאטא
ר"ל בלתי מוצלחת׳ פנים מכוכב כאשר הלבנה
בה עשה צלמי האבדון וההפסד וכל רעה׳ מתחיל
בסוף העמידה השלישית׳ ויוגבל במדרגה כ"א
משור.

הֹּ אַלמַיירַעם עמידה בלתי מוצלחת חמישית רעה
אדומה פנים מלבנה כאשר תרד הלבנה אליה עשה
צלמי כל התחברות רעות ותצליח׳ תתחיל בסוף
הרביעית ותוגבל במעלה הרביעית׳ ובחצית אומים
סוף שור וראש תאומים.

וֹּ אלטַיהִיאָך פנים ממארים מוצלח ארום׳ כאשר
היתה הלבנה בה עשה צלמי השלום ואהבה׳
מתחיל בסוף החמישי ויוגבל במדרגה י"ז מתאומים
והוא בטן תאומים.

וֹ אָדוּנְטוֹ פנים מצדק מוצלח מעורב לבן ואדום·
כאשר היתה הלבנה בו יעשה צלמי חיות ובהמות
השדה השלום והאהבה וכל טוב· מתחיל בסוף בתולה
וייגבל בסוף תאומים.

חֹ אַנְמֶרָאך הצלחה אדומה ולבנה פנים ממאדים
וכאשר הלבנה בו עשה צלמי המים הים והנהרות·
מתחיל בראש סרטן וייגבל במעלה י"ב ממנו
בעצמו.

טֹ אָאוּרָאט הצלחה לבנה פנים מחמה עשה בו
צלמי כל העופות· מתחיל בסוף השמינית וייגבל
במעלה כ"ה מסרטן גוף סרטן.

יֹ אַלַנְיָאַרְך הצלחה לבנה פנים מנוגה כאשר תרד
עליו הלבנה עשה צלמי הזאבים והשועלים וכל
החיות· מתחיל בסוף התשיעית וייגבל במעלה ח'
מארי' והיא סוף סרטן וראש ארי'.

יֹא אַבָּאָראב הצלחה שחורה פנים מכוכב כאשר
היתה בו הלבנה עשה צלמי ההפסד וההפלה
הקישור והניאוף וההפרש· מתחיל בסוף עשירי
וייגבל במעלה כ"א מארי' והוא גוף הארי'.

יֹב אַזַרָא הצלחה לבנה פנים מלבנה· כאשר
תרד עליו הלבנה עשה צלמי האהבה וחברה וכל טוב·
מתחיל בסוף י"א וייגבל במעלה ה"ד מבתולה
סוף ארי' וראש בתולה.

9

יָג אַלַנָק הצלחה לבנה פנים משבתי· כאשר תרד עליו הלבנה עשה צלמי האהבה· ולכל אשר תחפוץ השגתו· מתחיל· בסוף הי"ב וייגבל במעלה י"ז מבתולה בטן הבתולה.

יָד אַבָּמֶך הצלחה לבנה ואדומה וכוכב נבחר פנים מצדק· כאשר תרד עליו הלבנה עשה צלמי השתרגות והטיה· וכל ידידות ואהבה· מתחיל בסוף הי"ג וייגבל במעלה אחרונה מבתולה סוף בתולה.

טוֹ אַלְנָבַאשִים הצלחה לבנה פנים ממאדים כאשר תרד עליו הלבנה עשה צלמי צרה ורע לכל אשר תחפוץ· מתחיל בסוף הי"ד וייגבל במעלה י"ב ממאזנים.

יוֹ אַנְהָנִי הצלחה רעה פנים מחמה· כאשר הלבנה בו עשה צלמי ההפלה והאבדון והקשור· מתחיל בסוף הט"ו וייגבל במעלה כ"ה ממאזנים בטן מאזנים.

יוֹ אַליכִיל הצלחה רעה פנים מנוגה· כאשר הלבנה בו עשה צלמי המריבה וכל רע· מתחיל בסוף הי"ו וייגבל במעלה ח' מעקרב סוף מאזנים וראש עקרב.

יֹח אַשְיָבַּארֶך לב עקרב והצלחה לבנה פנים מכוכב· כאשר תרד עליו הלבנה עשה צלמי כל

טוב וקשור הלשונות והשתיקה· מתחיל בסוף הי"ז
וייגבל במעלה כ"א מעקרב.

יְט אלקאלב הצלחה רעה פנים מלבנה· כאשר
הלבנה בו עשה צלמי הניאוף והאריבה וקשור
הרצון· מתחיל בסוף הי"ח וייגבל במעלה הד'
מקשת תחילת קשת וסוף עקרב.

כ אַנאמֵי הצלחה לבנה פנים משבתי· כאשר
הלבנה בו עשה צלמי התעוררות השלום אהבה
וידידות· מתחיל בסוף הי"ט וייגבל במעלה י"ז
מקשת· בטן הקשת.

כְּא שַׁלְבְּרַאך הצלחה טובה פנים מצדק· כאשר
הלבנה בו עשה צלמי הטיה ושתיקה· מתחיל בסוף
הכ' וייגבל במעלה אחרונה מקשת סוף קשת.

כְּב שַׁדַאדְבֶּד הצלחה רעה פנים ממאדים·
כאשר הלבנה בו עשה צלמי כל רע· מתחיל
בתחלת גדי וייגבל במעלה י"ב ממנו בטן הגדי.

כְּג שַׁדָבּולַא הצלחה טובה פנים מחמה· כאשר
הלבנה בו עשה צלמי כל טוב· מתחיל בסוף
הי"ב וייגבל במעלה כ"ה סוף גדי וראש דלי
ויפורש הצלחת ההצלחות.

כְּד שַׁדַפַלַאטוך הצלחה טובה פנים מנוגה·
כאשר הלבנה בו עשה צלמי כל טוב· מתחיל
בסוף הכ"ג וייגבל במעלה ח' מדלי.

כֹּה שַׁדְלִיגִינְאַךּ פנים מכוכב הצלחה לבנה ·
כאשר הלבנה בו עשה צלמי כל שתיקה וקישור ·
מתחיל בסוף הכ"ד ויוגבל במעלה כ"א מרלי ·
בטן הדלי.

כֹּו אַלְגְרָאש הצלחה טובה פנים מלבנה · כאשר
הלבנה בו עשה צלמי ההשתרגות הדמיה
והידידות · מתחיל בסוף הכ"ה ויוגבל במעלה ר'
מרגים סוף דלי וראש דגים.

כֹּז אַלְפְרָאג האחרון הצלחה רעה ארומה פנים
משבווי · כאשר תרד עליו הלבנה עשה צלמי
ההפרשה וקשור וכל חולי · מתחיל בסוף הכ"ז
ויוגבל במעלה ו' מרגים בטן דגים.

כֹּח אַלְבֶטֶן הצלחה לבנה פנים מצדק · כאשר
הלבנה בו עשה צלמי כל טוב שתחפוץ · וכל מה
שיישיר אל השלמות · ותשלימהו כגזרת הבורא ית' ·
מתחיל בסוף הכ"ז ויוגבל במעלה אחרונה מרגים
סוף דגים.

מן הסמים

הנה הסמים אשר בם יעושנו כל צלמי הטוב
השתרגות וידידות הם אלי עץ אלוְאי אלבימום
שאפרם פָּילוַים ר"ל אַצְר · מכל אחד יוקח חלק
רביעי וישתמש בו או הלואד ר"ל עץ טוב

אזומרי ר"ל עץ מזימריא והוא אי אחד במדינות
האנדיא וזאפראן פילוווש ואֵזֶן מכל א' רביע אונקי.

Fol. 3 a.
הסמים אשר בם יעושנו צלמי הרעה
והמחלוקה והפירוד הם אלו· אלמַשך אלאפּֿור
אַצֶבַראלֹא שִיאֶר מֶֿרִיאטֵאַגֶֿראל אֲלֵידַנַאם · מכל
אחד יוקח חלק רביעי מאונקי וכולם ישתמשו·
אלַנַאק אֶלֻיזֶפּֿר אֲזֶכַרא לַוַאטֵי שְׁרֵיאדו שַׁלְֿיַא
שַׁנדל אַלַדֵינֶר אַלוֹאֶש שחור.

אמר בֵּלֵאנוֹם הפלוסוף כי ראשונה הי' צורך
השמות משעות היום והלילה כי יחויב להתפלל
בהם ולבקש העזר בכח טבעם וחזקם בגזרת
הבורא ית'.

דע כי השעה **הֹאֵ** מכל יום תקרא יובְּיטֻֿום
נ"א יַבַּֿאן ובה יתפללו בני אדם לפני בוראם·
והוא שעת קשור הלשונות מכל אדם.

הֹב תקרא גָאורנוֹרֵים נ"א גֶנורֵים ובה יתפללו
המלאכים לפני בוראם· ובה יעשה צלם הידידות
והשלום בין כל היצורים ובני אדם והתחברות
דעותם נ"א רוחתם.

הֹג תקרא בֶּנֹור נ"א בַּמפוּר בה יתנו תודה
העופות ליוצרם· בה יעשה צלם הדגים וכל
העופות ר"ל היונות (בני יונה).

13

הדֿ תקרא צְלָבִים נ"א צֵל גֵהִים בה יתנו
הברואים תודה לבוראם · בה יעשה צלמי הנחשים
והעקרבים.

הֿדֿ תקרא צְאֶלֶךְ נ"א צְלָלֶךְ בה יתנו כל הב"ח
הברואים תודה ליוצרם · בה יעשה צלמי החיות
והזאבים.

הֿוֿ תקרא צְיַדְמָהוּר נ"א מֶהֶמוּר · בה יתפלל
כְרוּבִי (לא ידעתי מהו) כסבת חטאות בני האדם
יעשו בה צלמי האסורים והחורין.

הֿוֿ תקרא יַידוּר בה יתפללו הכרובים נושאי
הכסא בה יעשו צלמי השלום בין המלכים והשרים.

הֿדֿ תקרא יַפּוֹרֵים נ"א יַפּוֹאִים · בה יעשו צלמי
הפירוד והמחלוקת בין בני אדם.

הֿטֿ תקרא בַא נ"א בַּרוֹן · בה יעשו צלמי ההולכי
דרכים להנצל מהמוקשים והעושקים ולא יעלו
נגדם לעולם.

הֿיֿ תקרא יַהִים נ"א יַכוּן · בה יזמרו המים
ליוצרם שירד בם רוח אלקים בהגבהת עיניהם ·
בה יעשו צלמי אוסרים המלכים ושרים כאשר
יכנס אליהם שלא ידברו אליו רעה אם בשעה
ההיא יהי' עמו.

הִיא תקרא יְבָרִים נ"א יֶהְרִים · בה יגילו
הצדיקים ובה יעשו צלמי הידידות אהבה ושלום.

הִיב תקרא בַצַלוֹם נ"א בַצַלוֹן · בה יעשו צלמי
השתיקה שלא ידברו לנצח אותם אשר תעשה
להם המעשה.

משמות שעות הלילה וצלמיהם.

והם יותר בעלי כח ומשובחים על הרוב
מאותם הנעשים ביום.

הַשָׁעָה הָאֹ מכל לילה תקרא אַמָן נ"א
בַּגַּם · בה יעשו תפלות השדים אל בוראם ואז לא
יוליד מכשול לשום אדם עד ישובו מתפלתם · בה
יעשו צלמי השתיקה.

הִיב תקרא תַמְבֵּיָ נ"א טִיבְזֶמִיר · בהי זמרו הרגים
ליוצרם וכל הב"ח אשר במים והרמש אשר בארץ
ובה יעשו צלמי הדגים ומושכי הדם והצפרדעים
וכל הב"ח אשר במים שלא יתנועעו ממקומם.

הִיג תקרא תַתוֹר נ"א בַהוֹר · בה יזמרו הב"ח
ליוצרם בה יעשו צלמי האש שלא ישרוף · ונחשים
ושרפים שלא יזיקו ובה יוקשרו בני אדם לבלתי
דבר.

15

הד תקרא אַלַאהִיר׳ בה ירחפו השדים על
הקברים ומזה יקרה מכשול כי אם ימצא שם
איזה אדם יפחד ושעריו יסתמרו כיענה והשתוממות
ובה יעשו הצלמים ויפותחו מזהב אל השלום ואהבה
עזה והוא צלם העליה.

הה תקרא כמייפֿוּר׳ בה ינוחו המים ויזמרו
לבוראם׳ בה יעשו צלמי העננים והרוחות הבלתי
נאותות.

הו תקרא זַוּם נ״א צַרוּרִי׳ בה ינוחו המים ויעמדו
גם שיהיו נגרשים ואם בשעה הזאת בעצמו
יימשחו בם אחר שיעורב במשיחה בעלי הקדחות
אשר ימנע מאתם השנה יבואם שינה וינוח׳
בגזרת הבור׳׳ ובה יעשו צלמי החלומות אשר בם
יראה כל מה שראוי לעשות בענייני העולם בחלום.

הז תקרא יַפֿוֹר נ״א יַפֵֿר׳ בה יעשו צלמי המלכים
והשרים אם ישאל מהם דבר ישיגנו ולא ישיבו
פניו ריקם בשום דבר לעולם.

הח תקרא זִימַלַי׳ בה יתנו תודה זרעי הארץ
ליוצרם׳ בה יעשו צלמי הגנות והפרדסים אילנות
וכל זרעי הארץ שיצליחו וישומרו מכל נזק כרצון
הבורא ית׳.

הט תקרא צְפַֿר נ״א זַפַֿרים׳ בה יתפללו המלאכים
אל ה׳ לקשור העולם׳ בה יעשו צלמים לפני מלכים

ושרים לקשור עניני רצון האדם וכל הברואים ולרחות נזקם.

הִי֗ תקרא נַהֲלָקו נ"א מַלְכו והיא רב התועלת' בה יעשו צלמים שימנעו כל נשי המדינה מניאוף או איזה אשה בפרט.

הִֽיא֗ אַלְכו נ"א אַלְתו' בה יפתחו שערי השמים כאשר יקרא בה האדם אל בוראו יותן לו כל משאלותיו באמונה' ובה יעשו צלמי השלום החזק והאהבה אשר לא תוסר והזיווגים ותקרא ג"כ אִינְדִינו והיא על פני כל הארץ ובה יתפלל השמש אל יצורי הבורא העליון ממעון קדשו.

הִי֗ב תקרא שֶׁלֶם נ"א שְׁלָלֶם ובה ינוחו צבא השמים עד יתפללו בני אדם לבוראם העליון' ובה יעשו צלמי השתיקה והפרישות ויקרא צלם ההשתוממות והפחד אשר יביט אליו יבהל וירעד כחסר הדעת ולא יהיה לו היכולת על הדיבור' וכל מה שיעשה בשעה זו לא יוסר מאחד לנצח והוא בחון אמנם הצלמים האלו יֵעֲשׂו מד' מיני מתכות מבדיל זהב נחושת כסף.

פני המזלות.

כל מזל יחלק לג' חלקים שוים' וכל חלק הוא מי' מעלות' ויקרא פנים' ואם תדע המעלה

Fol. 4 α.

17

בצומחת מהם התבונן איזה שעה היא · והמעלה
אשר המזל בה חשוך ט"ו מעלות צומחים.

תמונת שבתי · · צדק · · מאדים
חמה · · נוגה · · כוכב · · לבנה. · ·

See plate.

פנים צומח כאשר ביום א' או בתחילת
היום יכנס המזל והוא מתחבר בשרביט החמה ·
בהיות החמה ולבנה כמזל אחד · והחבור ההוא
נקרא הצלחה צומחת או צמיחת ההצלחה ר"ל
פורטונא.

מצלמי שעות היום.

אמר כלינוס כי הצלם הראשון יעשה בשעה
ראשונה מכל יום לקשור כל הלשונות שלא ידברו
רע לעולם · הנה יותך צלם אשר חציו כסף וחציו
בדיל ושיהיה הלבנה ד' עשוי על דמות אדם
ובשעה ראשונה מהיום ויפותח בראשו שם בעל
הצלם ההוא · ובחזה שם השעה ראשונה מהיום
ההוא · וכבבטנו אלו השמות בָּלַךְ רָלַךְ ותקברהו
בפתחו וזה הקשור בחון על כל הלשונות וענים
ולבבות · וכתוב בחזה שלו שם החמה והלבנה
ושם מלאכי החלק ההוא אשר בו יעשו הצלם.
וטמן כתוב על השדרה מהצלם ושמות מפוארים
אשר בם ברא הבורא ית' שמים וארץ וים וכל
אשר בו' · וכתוב בכח שמות למנוע ולקשור את

הלשונות מי שתרצה בין מבני אדם ויתר הב"ח
והעופות׳ וחקוק בכל א׳ מהם לעצמו מלאכיו
והשמות אשר תפתח הם אלו ואם תקראם ג"כ
לכל מה שתרצה לדחות ידחה ותקראם בהיפוך׳
לַמְטָרוֹרוּשׁ לַלְכִיסּ לַנְפוֹרִישׁ לַנְגְבָּאלִי לַשָׁפָּם וֶזָל
לַשָׁפָּט וכי אלו השמות פעולתם על כל פנים
יקשור בהם כל אשר יחפוץ או למנוע את אשר
תחפוץ׳ וגם להתיר בם בעצמם׳ אמנם כאשר
יכוון לעשות צלם הקשור והמניעה יקראו ראשונה
אלו השמות כסדר בזמן פתוח הצלם׳ אולם אם
יכוון לעשות צלם הדחי׳ יקראו השמות על סדר
היפוך באופן שלא יהי׳ חפועל המכוון לריק ואלו
השמות נעלמים מכל׳ אמנם הזהר אם תשלים
הפעל מאיזו צלם שבשעה שיפותח בה השמות תבטא
שם הדבר אשר תחפוץ בקשורו׳ אם כפר או כרך
או עיר או מדינה או שררה או זיווג איש אשה
בהמות חיות עופות עננים רוחות׳ ובכלל כל אשר
תקשור או תחפוץ למנוע כפי האופן הנזכר תקרא
השמות בעצמם ותצליח.

הצלם השני.

יעשה שעה ב׳ מכל יום ונקרא צלם
ההשתרגות והשלום האמיתי׳ יעשה צלם מכסף
וכדיל עם ראשים (נ"ל צור) נתכים ובשעה ההיא
יפותחו בראשיהם שמות בעליהם ובחזה שם בעל
השעה ובבטניהם יכתבו אלו השמות׳ בַהֲלִים

מְדוּאָלִים מָנוּפָּקוֹן פַּרִיאוֹלָם נַלְבַּטָן בְּרָהֲרִים וְכַאשר
נעשו ב' הצלמים כאשר נזכר יחופרו בחזה שלהם
עם שעות משובחת' אח"כ שימהו בבית כל א'
מהם ר"ל האיש והאשה אשר חפצת לעוררם אל
האהבה' באופן שיעברו עליהם ויהי' ביניהם
אהבה אשר לא תופר.

הצלם השלישי.

יעשה בשעה השלישית מהיום ויקרא צלם
קשור כל הדגים והעופות' הנה יעשה צלם מאיזה
דג או עוף שתחפץ' ושמות מלאכי השעה יפותחו
בבטנו אח"כ יעושן אם אַלְוָא ירוק ושנדלו אדום
ויקבר במקום בעצמו אשר לו הצלם עשוי אם
יעשה צלם דג יקבר במים ויראה אז נפלאות
מרצון הדברים הנשמעים לדבר ההוא בעצמו
בגזרת הבורא ית'.

הצלם הרביעי.

יעשה שעה ד' מהיום ויקרא צלם העקרבים
נחשים שרפים וכל הרמשים המזיקים' ויאמר
ג"כ צלם מחיות שונות' הנה יעשה שעה הנ"ל
וכתוב על ראש הצלם שם החי אשר תחפוץ לקשרו
ושם מלאך השעה בבטנה' ובחזה שלו יכתבו
השמות המפוארים מהשעה הראשונה ויקבר במקום
בעלי חיים מהמין ההוא בעצמו אשר נעשה לו

הצלם הזה וכל עוד שיעמוד הצלם שם לא יוכלו
עוד מהמין ההוא לצאת.

הצלם החמישי.

יעשה שעה ה' מהיום ויקרא צלם הזאבים
והשועלים והארנביות ויתר הב"ח הדומים לאלו׳
ויעשה מכסף על תמונת הב"ח אשר חפצת
בקשורו ויפותח שם הב"ח ושם ממונה השעה
בחזה ושמות השעה הראשונה בבטנו׳ ויעושן עם
אלוֹא ושנדלו אדום ויקבר במקום מעבר המין ההוא
ויצליח.

הצלם השישי.

יעשה שעה ו' מהיום הנקרא צלם האסורים
ושבויים׳ ויעשה בצורת איש או אשה מבדיל או
כסף׳ ויכתוב בראשו שם האיש או אשה ושם
בעל השעה בחזה׳ ושמות שעה ראשונה בבטנו
ויעושן׳ אח"כ ינתן לאיש או אשה אשר נעשה
בעבורו ויותר באותו היום׳ וכן יעשה לקשור מים
אשר תחפוץ בקשורים ותצליח בעזר הבורא ית'.

הצלם השביעי.

יעשה שעה ז' מהיום מועיל להכנס לפני
שרים ומלכים וישיג בו אהבה עזה וכבוד רב

מאוד · ויעשה צלם מכסף ויפותח על ראשו שם
המלך וכן בבטנו שמות השעה ה"א ובהכנסו לפני
המלך ישא הצלם הזה עמו וישיג כל חפצו ברצון
הבורא.

הצלם השמיני.

יעשה שעה ח' מהיום ויקרא צלם האבדון
ודחית בני האדם שלא יעמדו בבית או מדור בשום
פע' ויעשה צלם מנחשת אדום עם שני ראשים
אשר האחד ראש אדם והשני ראש חמור · וכתוב
על ראשו שם האומה או האדם או משפחה ·
ושם בעל השעה בחזה · ושמות השעה הראשונה
בבטנו ותעשנהו עם דם אדם הנהרג וחלבו וקברהו
במקום אשר חפצת לדחות ממנו אותם אשר
בעבורם נעשה הצלם ההוא ותראה ממנו נפלאות
בגזרת הבורא ית'.

הצלם התשיעי.

יעשה שעה ט' מהיום לקשור הגזלנים ·   Fol. 5 a.
ויעשה צלם אדם מכסף וכתוב שמו בראשו ושמות
מלאכי האפלה בחזה ושמות השעה ה"א בבטנו ·
ועשנהו עם אלואי מנוקה וכרכום ושאהו עמך
ויבהלו הגזלנים ויעשו כחסרי הדעת · ותנצל מידם
בגזרת העליון ית'.

הצלם העשירי.

יעשה צלם בשעה י' ההשתרגות וידידות בין
שנים אשר ביניהם שנאה· ויעשה ב' צלמים בשעה
י"א מהיום מכסף נבחר או בדיל שוה משקלם
וכתוב שמותיהם בראשיהם· ובחזה שלהם שם
בעל השעה ובבטנם שם השעה ראשונה· ועשן
אותם עם אלואי מנוקה וכרכום וחברם יחד וקברם
באש בלתי חזק ויבא אליך בסבר פנים יפות בכל
מקום שתחפוץ.

הצלם האחד עשר.

יעשה בשעה י"א והוא לחזק ולקים ולהוליד
אהבת כל בני האדם וידידות· יעשה צלם מכסף
כדמות אדם וכתוב שמו בראש ושם בעל השעה
בחזה· ושמות מלאכי האהבה והקשור בבטן ועשנהו
עם אלואי לבן וכרכום ושאהו עמך בבגד משי
לבן ותשיג כל מה שתתפוץ.

הצלם השני עשר.

יעשה בשעה י"ב לקשור הלשונות· עשה
צלם מבדיל על צורת איזה שתחפוץ· וחקוק שמו
בראשו ושם בעל השעה בחזה· ובבטנו שמות השעה
הראשונה והקשור· ועשנהו בעץ אלואי מנוקה·

23

וכרכום' אח"כ קברהו תחת מפתן פתח הבית עד
יעבור עליו אותו אשר חפצת' אח"כ שימהו
בבגד משי לבן ושאהו עמך' וכתוב בשדרה
מצלם ההשתוממות' ואלו השמות נעלמים אצל
החכמים' אחר זה תעשנהו וטרם תקברהו אמור
ההשבעה הזאת' אשביע אתכם שמות הקדושים
בשם הקודש אשר ככחם תבעירו אותם ותפרוט
כל אחד בשמו שַׁמַלְיאִיל שְׁנִיאוֹל אַנְשָׁרוֹשׁ אָרִישׁ
טָלִיק אוּמָאִילְרָבָא מָאִיל אָבְּרָא שׁוּאַשׁ אַבְרְהִי לָבְּרַנְשׁ
הַצִּיוֹן מָמוֹר וְטוּפָרוֹן אַפְנָתַם מַנְשָׁא הָאָרְקוֹד אֶל
אִישְׁטַאיִל אַבְּירִיל בְּלַיאַר וְמֵר אֶל אַבְרֵי אָאִיר
דוּרְקוּמִינְט וְנַשׁ שִׁיאַר מְיַר אַטוֹאַמְכָן שָׁאבְּשֶׁאָאוּשׁ
שׁוּפָא אוֹ כִּילַאשׁ אח"כ תעשנהו עם מֵלוֹ אַנַבְק
וַנֶגֶרַשׁ תחת המערכה השביעית מהלילה כדברך
עליו שמות.

מצלמי הלילה.

הצלם הראשון יעשה שעה א' מהלילה'
כמעשה חמרחצאות והשתיקה אמר כְּאָלִינוֹם כאשר
בקש ממנו אחד להכין לו מרחץ וכו' קח ברזל
או נחשת מותך ועשה ממנו מנורה ר"ל כלי אשר
לו ז' פיות' וכתוב על כל א' מהפיות השמות
האלו' צְפָבַצָטִין שֶׁצֶשִׁין הַיָפֵשִׁין בְּרָהִין בַּלִין שְׁשָׁהִין   Fol. 5 b.
ובכל פה יהי' פתילה א' טוחה בשמן וכתוב
בחלק התחתון מהכלי אלו השמות הנעלמים אשר
הם מהשתוממות נוּרִין בַּלְדְכִין זָהִיר יַאפוּנִין אַלְכֵר

בַּאדִיכִין אַנדִין בַּאדִין שְׁנִיכִין' וַעַשׂה עַל הַכְּלִי
הַנַ"ל צְלֶם מנְחשֶׁת עַל צוּרַת אִישׁ אֲשֶׁר בְּיָדוֹ נֵר
נחשת אוֹ פַךְ כְּאֵלוּ יִשְׁפּוֹךְ שֶׁמֶן בַּלְתֵי מְהוּפַךְ כְּלִי'
וכָתוֹב עַל פְּנֵי הַצְלֶם הַשֵּׁמוֹת הָאֵלוּ הַשְּׁנַיִם
בַּמְרַאיֵל לַאוּדְפַּיִל וכֵן עַל הַבֶּטֶן וְבַתַחַתִית הַכְּלִי
(מאדים and שַׁבְתֵּי signs of) וְסָגוֹר אוֹ טַמוֹן פָּנָיו
שֶׁלֹא יִפַּתַח לַנֵצַח.

הצלם השני.

יַעֲשָׂה לַמְנִיעַת הַנִיאוּף' אֲמַר כַּאלִינוּס נכְנַסְתִּי
לַעִיר נִקְרָא לַאיבָר וְעָלֵיהָ תִּקַנְתִּי צְלֶם שֶׁלֹא תִּנְאַף
בָּה אִשָּׁה לְעוֹלָם וכֵן הִי' עַשָׂה צֶלֶם מנְחֶשֶׁת
מנוּקָה וכָתוֹב עָלֵיו אֵלוּ הַשֵׁמוֹת פֵּלְבָּלַךְ הוֹרְמוֹרֶשׁ
רַיְשַׁנָק שִׁיקוֹלִים זוּוַנּוּר בַּמְיַנַךְ וכָתוֹב הַשֵׁמוֹת
הָאַחַרִים עַל טֶם נחשת וְשִׂים הַטֶם בְּיַד הַצְלֶם
הַהוּא לְהַחַזִיקוּ זַבְּמַנִי וֶלַמַנִי שׁוּבַרְבִים אִינוּכָּיֵאל אוֹ
מוּכָּיֵאל נוּכָּיִאוֹן שׁוּשַׁנִיאוֹן אַבַּ' אח"כ יִקַבַּר הַצְלֶם
בָּעִיר כַּפַר אוֹ בֵית אֲשֶׁר תַחַפּוֹץ וִישָׁלִים בִּגְזוּרַת
הַבּוֹרֵא ית' וכֵן תוּכַל לַעֲשׂוֹת בְּדָגִים וְצִפַרְדְעִים וכָל
שַׁרְצֵי הָעוֹלָם.

הצלם השלישי.

יַעֲשָׂה שָׁעָה ג' מֵהַלַיְלָה לִדְחוֹת כָּל ב"ח הַמַזִיקִין
כְּמוֹ נחָשִׁים עַקְרָב' כְּלָבִים עַכְבָּרִים וִיהוּדוֹמִים יַעֲשָׂה
צְלֶם מנְחֶשֶׁת עַל אֵיזֶה ב"ח שַׁתַרְצֶה' וכָתוֹב עַל .

פניו אלו השמות· בגבול המקום· או במעבר ג'
דרכים· במדור אשר תחפוץ· ולא ישאר שמה ב"ח
דומה לצורת הצלם· ונטרוטון נ"א אובַמְרון בוריאון
נ"א בַּרַיַן פְֿרושימיאון פַֿרַרְיל רובוטון.

הצלם הרביעי.

יעשה שעה ד' מהלילה להחריב בית או
כפרים או עיירות· ולהשיב אחור כל עסק והשתדלות
שונאך· יקח מיץ מגמל וכתוב על פתח השונא
כולינְתָאוש וִינֶקְט פֿרָנְגל צֿידוריאון גִינְמַן ואמור
אשביע אתכם שתפסידו הבית או העסק או הדבר
פ' אשר לפלוני ויהיה כן.

הצלם החמישי.

יעשה שעה ה' מהלילה· להפסיד צבא עננים
או ברד ולהוליד מריבה בין בני האדם יעשו ב'
צלמים א' מעופרת וא' מנחשת אדום· שוי המשקל
דהיינו כ"א מ"ד ליטר'· וחקוק בהם הקרקטירי האלו

See plate.

ותעשנם ותאמר עליהם שמות המלאכים ותקברם
במקום היותר גבוה בעיר או כפר או בית ויפול
ביניהם שנאה או מחלוקת· צֿיתָאום פֶֿבִיל אולַכון
אולם אם חפצת להפסיד העננים ולרחות הב"ח
שתרצה· תקברם במקום היותר גבוה מהעיר או
מחצר או בית· ויושלם כרצון הבורא ית'.

הצלם השישי.

Fol. 6 a.

יעשה שעה ו' מהלילה מנחשת אדום ויקרא
צלם הדרחי' והגרוש' ויפותחו עליו שמות מלאכי
חדרחי' והגרוש האלו בְּלִיאָן בְּכִי אִי אַאולים
אַבְרַכִים אַפּוֹלֵנוּ הַדַלּוֹם או הַנְטִינַאָן וכתוב במצחו
שם אותו אשר חפצת לגרש מבית או עיר וקבר
הצלם במקום הנ"ל.

הצלם השביעי.

יעשה שעה ז' מהלילה ' לשרפת גפנים ואילנות
וכל מיני ירקות' עשה צלם מנחשת אדום וחקוק
עליו אלו השמות' וקברהו בגבול המדור וישרוף
נחלתם עד עשרה מילין' אַיר כַּמְנַת הַגְּרַנְאָן כָּבֶד
הוּבְרָה הַיִד מַתֵד מֵאוּרַתִי בַּפָּרְוָא אַדְרְצָר מַרְ ר"ל
אש משמים ישרוף שרפה לכבוד הבורא ית'

כשרפת * * * * אַבְלִינְלֵל See plate.
שרוף ברצון הבורא ית'.

הצלם השמיני.

יעשה שעה ח' מהלילה ' לחבר העופות ובני
יונים אשר סביבך מרחוק עשרה מילין עד תצוד
אותם' יעשה צלם אל צורת איזו עוף אשר תחפוץ
מזהב נבחר' משקלו מינראל אחד (.*mg* לא ידעתי)

27

ופתח בם אלו השמות· יַרְבַּק בַּתְנַךְ אָרוֹךְ אַכִילוּךְ
באו הנה העופות מכל מקום גבריאל יסיר אתכם
מכל צדדי עשרה מילין וקבור אותו במקום היותר
גבוה בעיר או כפר ויקובצו סביבו העופות ועל
אלו הפנים תוכל לעשות לכל בעל כנף אשר
חפצת כחבורו וקבוצו ברצון ה"ית.

הצלם התשיעי·

יעשה שעה ט' מהלילה לקבוץ כל העופות
באחד ההרים אשר תחפוץ· יעשה צלם על תמונת
איזה עוף שתרצה· מאונקי' א' מזהב ויהי' חלול
וחקוק בו השמות אשר למטה וקברהו במקום
היותר גבוה אשר שמה ויקובצו כולם מהמין ההוא
מרחוק עשרה מילין· ואלו הם השמות·

See plate.

שׁוּר בְּנִישׁוֹר מוּכַל מוּכָאֵל וַנָאֵשׁ רָל בָּא.

הצלם העשירי·

יעשה שעה י' להפריד האהובים שלא יהי'
שלום ביניהם עוד לנצח· יעשה צלם מבדיל וחלק
רביעי מנחשת אדום ארכו זרת אחד ר"ל פלמו אח"כ
עשה עוד צלם אחד דומה לזה· וכתוב על כל א'
שם אשר אותם אשר בעבורם עשית הצלמים
האלו ועל החזה שמות מלאכי הפירוד· ובשדרה

כתוב השמות אשר תראה אח"כ תעשנם וקבור
כל א' מהם ביחוד במקומות מתחלפות שלא
יתחברו וכן תוכל לעשות בדרך זה על כל אשר
תחפוץ להוליד מריבה ביניהם.

See plate.

הצלם האחד עשר.

יעשה שעה י"א מהלילה להביא או להסיר Fol. 6 *b*.
איש או אשה מאיזה מקום שתתחפוץ' יעשה צלמו
מאונקי' א' כסף או בדיל היותר יפה מתואר
שאפשר והקוק שמו על ראשו ובחזה שם השעה
הי"א והוא גברום ובבטנו כתוב אלו השמות
המפוארים ארוגיאון רַנִיאַל בְּבְנִי אִיצְכַלִיש לְשמְלִים
ברן לַרמַנָאָם גְרבקלון לְבַר הְלַלַאון פִימַרון שוִאַדִי
מָלון אח"כ קברהו באש חלוש ותבא אליך האשה
ההיא באותה הלילה אשר תצוה.

הצלם השני עשר.

יעשה שעה י"ב מהלילה לטווות הפנים
והרעדת הגוף' יעשה צלם מנחשת אדום על
דמות אותו אשר חפצת' והפנים יהפך מול השדרה
שלו ורגליו יהיו מול הידים וידיו במקום הרגלים
וכתוב שמו בראשו ובגבו שמות ההשתוממות
וקברהו לפני פתח ביתו יבהל הגוף ההוא וירעד

29

ויהי׳ כמשוגע כל זמן שהצלם ההוא מהופך׳ או
שימהו תחת עץ אַלכַינְיָא נ״א אַלכַמֶד ויהי׳ סכלו
על אחת עשרה מבראשונה ואלו הם השמות׳
אַרדַפַגו הום אַלִין אַוּגֵ מַאַר שדה קַבֲלַש מַלַש מַתָה
תוּאָרום תַל דובֲילִין׳

נשלמו צלמי היום והלילה.

מעשה הצלמים כפי פֶטוֹלֶמָאו והוא יותר
אמתי ומיוחד בנסיון מכל הצדדים הנשארים׳ אשר
פעלו מסודר על פנים מצלמי המזלות׳ אמר
אלבוּבֲקֵר כאשר האנשים המזרחיים יעשו הצלמים
האלו לא ישימו לב על אחרים׳ רק יזהרו שהצומח
יהי׳ כארשטרופא בעת שיפעלו ואז יצליחו.

תם ונשלם

שבח לאל

בורא עילם.

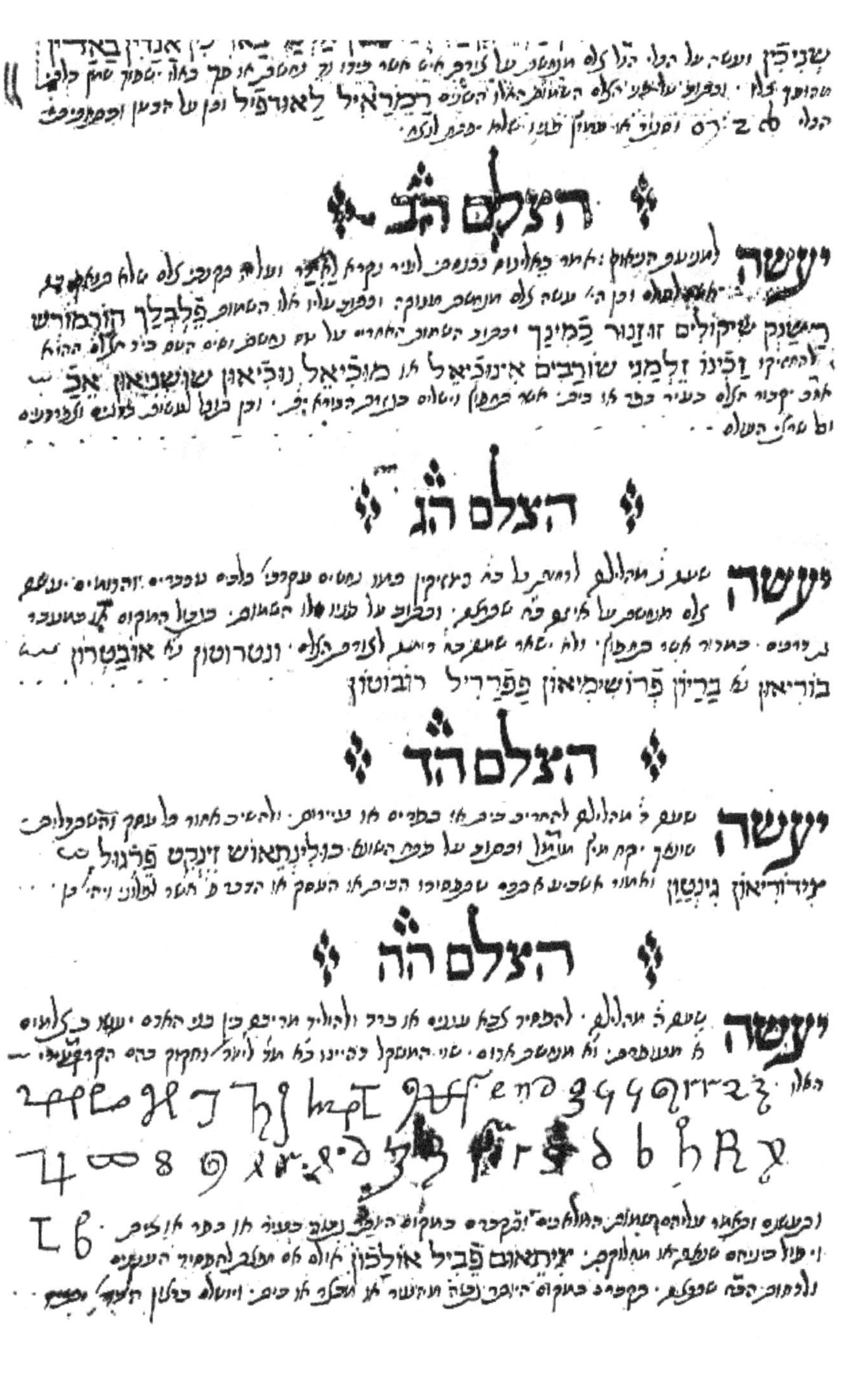
הצלם הב׳
עשה
הצלם הג׳
עשה
הצלם הד׳
עשה
הצלם הה׳
עשה

צלם

Figure 12: *Sepher ha- Levanah*, plate 6a, showing pages 24-5
(The Second Image to the Fifth Image)

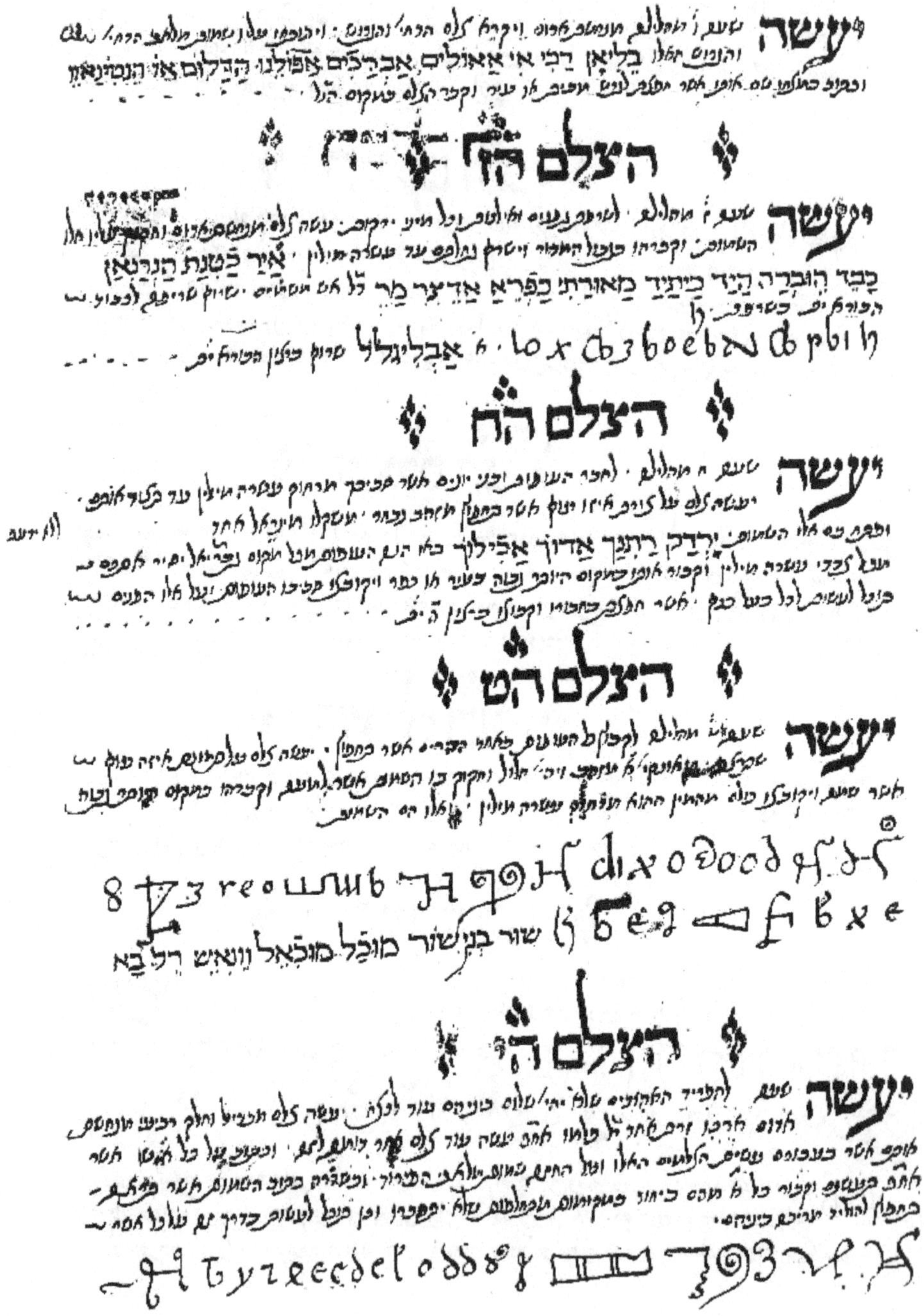

Figure 13: *Sepher ha- Levanah*, plate 6b, showing pages 26-8
(The Seventh Image to the Tenth Image)

SEPHER HA–LEVANAH

English translation by Calanit Nachshon
edited and annotated by Don Karr

EDITOR'S INTRODUCTION

Reverend A. W. [Albert William] Greenup, D.D. (1866-1952) was principal of the London College of Divinity, Church of England, (now St. John's College, Nottingham) from 1899 to 1925. He is known to us through his translations of rabbinic literature, the best circulated being *The Mishna Tractate Taanith (On the Public Feasts)* (London: Palestine House, 1918) and, to a lesser extent, *Sukkah, Mishna and Tosefta* (London: Society for Promoting Christian Knowledge/New York: Macmillan, 1925). His earliest publications, *The Targum on the Book of Lamentations* (Sheffield: Sheffield Academic Press, 1893) and *A Short Commentary on the Book of Lamentations: Chapter I: For the Use of Students* (Herford: Stephen Austin & Sons, 1893) were written while Greenup was still an M.A. Among his last published pieces are 'A Kabbalistic Epistle by R. Isaac b. Samuel b. Hayyim Sephardi,' in *Jewish Quarterly Review*, VOLUME 21 NEW SERIES (Philadelphia: Dropsie College for Hebrew and Cognate Learning, 1931: English introduction, Hebrew text), and 'Feasts and Fasting,' in *Essays in Honour of the Very Rev. Dr. J. H. Hertz*, edited by Isadore Epstein, Joseph Herman Hertz, Ephraim Levine, and Cecil Roth (London: E. Goldston, 1942).

Greenup's 1912 edition of *Sepher ha-Levanah*, referred to with such noticeable frequency in books and articles which touch upon magic, was notoriously hard to locate and cite directly until Joseph H. Peterson posted the introduction and title page on his website, TWILIT GROTTO—ESOTERIC ARCHIVES, as "A. W. Greenup: Sefer ha-Levanah—The Book of the Moon,"[98] and published scans of the text and plates on his CD, *Esoteric Archives: 48*

---

[98] www.esotericarchives.com/levanah/levanah.htm. Peterson writes, "The book is extremely rare. The only copy I could find is in the Cambridge University Library."

Our source copy of Greenup's *Sepher ha-Levanah* resides in the Hebraic Section of the African and Middle Eastern Division, Library of Congress, Washington, D.C.

Complete Books (Kasson: Twilit Grotto, 2000).[99] Unfortunately, Peterson's scans as published are not always clear enough to distinguish ב *beit* from כ *kaph*, ו *vav* from ז *zayin*, or final ם *mem* from ס *samekh*.

The text of *Sepher ha-Levanah* is in a knotty, inconsistent Hebrew. The clarity of the rendition offered below is due to the diligence and judgment of the translator, Calanit Nachshon. Fortunately, many passages of *Sepher ha-Levanah* and *Liber Lunæ* (along with passages from other portions of Sloane MS 3826) are quite similar, often mirroring each other in their odd ordering of words and phrases, particularly in their respective sections on the hours of the day and night. Thus, the English of Sloane MS 3826 informed the translation of *Sepher ha-Levanah*.

Greenup's transcription contains many errors. Since we have only two images of the original text (both showing "square" Hebrew, Rashi script, *and* a magical script), we cannot determine whether these mistakes reflect the original or Greenup's misreadings of it. One persistent error, for example, is that the speaker cited in several passages is given as כאלינוס, *Kelinos*, which, in all parallel sources is *Belenus* (or, as in *Liber Lunæ*, *Bolemus*): an instance of ב *beit* and כ *kaph* confused.

In comparing Greenup's *Sepher ha-Levanah* and the *Liber Lunæ* material in Sloane MS 3826, one is tempted to assume a common source, for the two match, part-for-part, with only a few exceptional paragraphs (which are described in my introduction to *Liber Lunæ*). But to really achieve this near-complete replication between the texts, we must look outside of the *Liber Lunæ* portion of Sloane MS 3826 to other parts of the MS (in particular *fols.* 78-80), and we must ignore *Liber Lunæ's* last major section (§ 4.), for *Sepher ha-Levanah* contains nothing on the figures of the planets. All the same, comparing the initial pages of the two texts one is struck by their similarity, from the preambles pronounced by Hermes to the MANSIONS OF THE MOON sections, in which both give only the name, portion of the zodiac, and brief indications regarding the "image"; in the MANSIONS section of neither are there any details on contructing talismans or on incantations.

Sepher ha-Levanah's § (3) [Fol. 2 *b ff.*], "On potions," is incorrectly described by Greenup as "Twelve directions as to the סמים [*samim - potions*] to be used for good and evil צלמים [*tzelemim - images*]." This section starts with two short paragraphs on *potions*, but seems more about *concoctions*. Parallel texts use the term *suffumigations*, as, for example, *Liber Lunæ fol.* 86v. Following this are

---

[99] A more recent edition of the CD "includes 50+ complete books [and] 31 complete grimoires."

"twelve directions," which say nothing about *potions* but rather give the names, virtues, and images of the hours of the day in a manner similar to Sloane MS 3826, *fols.* 78-78v.[100]

Nachshon's translation reflects the characteristics of Greenup's transcription, using different sized type faces, boldface, and italics, while generally following the Hebrew word choice and order. The odd mix of verb tenses has been retained,[101] along with some chopped clauses, repetitions, and free-floating phrases. Terms like *fortuna* and *infortunata*, which are characteristic of the Latin version, are kept as source indicators. We have also preserved the clumsiness — or *charm* — of the language, which befits this type and vintage of text.

---

[100] .See Supplements to *Liber Lunæ* § 3: b.
[101] The odd tenses may reflect the Hebrew translator's confusion with the moods of Latin verbs, in particular the *subjunctive*.

Sepher ha-Levanah

THE BOOK OF THE MOON

[Fol. 1 *b*]

(1)[102] **Said *Hermes*,**[103] [I have seen][104] all of the books written on the stars, all of them [which] are [written on the] planets. All the same, I have never found one which is more true and complete or superb than the one that the wise men called *The Book of the Moon*. And [in] the first part, therefore, I will exhort you before the Lord of Heaven that you will never give it over to anyone, and if something evil is derived from it, the Creator, blessed be He[105], will demand it from you. It will occasion good and evil operations on every day and [in every] month that you have desired, and it is a superior and important book which is proper to keep hidden. And it contains the ineffable name of God and by that [name] either a good or evil operation can be done. Therefore, you should fear God and keep yourself from defying His honor, God, blessed be He, and you shall not tell the secret to other people so that evil and desolation will never come out of it. And if you desire to gain [by] one of the images, [you should] steer away from any impurity so that your desire will be fulfilled by your deeds.

Here, when you desire to make one of the images, recite over it the names of the angels which were [written] below as you suffume it with fine ingredients seven times while stating everything that you desired. With it, the name of the hour, the name of the Moon, and also the name of the mansion, and by God, blessed be He, within the mansions under which you operate, there will be the Moon alone, with [its] divine assistance, etc.[106]

---

[102] Numbers in parentheses indicate section numbers given in Greenup's INTRODUCTION.

[103] Greenup does not seem to recognize that הרמס is Hermes. The MS being under the authority of Hermes would indicate the likely Greek/Alexandrian origin of the text.

[104] Throughout the text, words within brackets are my additions; parenthetical remarks are part of the translation.

[105] Greenup's transcription shows the abbreviation ית׳, which could also be "God will save us," "God will exalt," or "God will have mercy."

[106] The paragraphs on this page closely parallel the second paragraph of *Liber Lunæ* (*fols.* 84r-84v), not just in content and general form but also in the order of words and phrases.

These are the names of the angels who serve the Moon—which is to say the images of the Moon and its cycle, which you will swear upon seven times over every image with each suffumigation that is [described] below, whether these are good operations or evil ones. And these are the words of the angels [with] whose secrets you should improve your understanding, and you will keep them [hidden] with extreme diligence:

Anailim, Quntzilim, Gashgorzim, Aqashimadi, Amikhilim, Abrakiim, Abrashim, Lairayozim, Yamaghash, Manenim, Mangororam, Hartninay, Montaginim, Latzandonim, Qamshilindim, Shaamam, Sharailim, Amaamilim, Haqoilim, Balknaritim, Arihaylim, Beqshdeilim, Abranodomilim, Qarmayndim, Andalashim, Sharahitzinim, Adiamenim, Tzetahotim, Yatzarpnishim, Teibinenim, Nehelim. Hiraminim, Abramatim, Lanagotim, Wipoliyaqa, Belgahalidim, Gaporim, Aqrapirim[1], Tayriomim, Diqomeylim, Genithokim, Madarilim, Kearldim, Yebrunkhelim, Aladim, Yadalim, Shethakam, Panaplor, Badaylin, Dabnotirorin.[2]

(2) **Said** *Kelinos*[3], Exactly when the Moon is in *Beanakh*, or *Elanakh* in another version, which is the first mansion, when it is full you should recite [the names of] its cycle. And it is the face of Mars, and [in it] you will make the images of discord and hatred.

1. And that mansion will be the first face of Aries. And it starts at the head of Aries and is limited to twelve degrees within Aries, and [another] half [degree in] Aries. It is its head.[4]

2. *Albizaqin*, or *Albuqiim* in another version, white *fortuna*, the face of the Sun and *fortunata* (which is to say [a] fortun[ate]) mansion. When the Moon descends in it, [operations are] made [of] hope, of returning, the

---

[1] Throughout this translation, an unitalicized "p" is used where the letter *peh* is shown with a line over it in (ᵽ) Greenup's text.

[2] There are 50 names here, surely parallel to the 55 angels in *Liber Lunæ* (86v) and the 54 angels noted by Thorndike, *History of Magic*, VOL 2, page 223.

[3] It appears that *kaph* has replaced *beit*; the name here should be "Belenus." This misspelling, or misreading, occurs throughout. In *Liber Lunæ*, this name appears as "Bolemus."

This section, through the 28 numbered paragraphs, parallels *Liber Lunæ* § 1 (84v-86v).

[4] This paragraph should not have been separated from the previous one, starting "Said *Kelinos*."

purchase of love[1] and friendship. It starts at twelve degrees within Aries and is limited to twenty six degrees within it.[2] And it is the belly of Aries.

3. *Aqhoranay*, or *Alturayib* in another version, which means to say the end of Aries and the head of Taurus and [the] white face. And *fortuna* [i.e., good fortune] from Venus. When the Moon was in it, the image of words of grace [are made], and the things you desired to join together should be made. And it is in the end of the second mansion and is limited to eight degrees within Taurus.

4. *Aldebaram* (mg. fire)[3] - is *infortunata* [i.e., an unfortunate] mansion - which means to say the unfortunate face of Mercury. When the Moon is in it, make the images of desolation, loss, and every evil. It begins at the end of the third mansion and is limited to twenty one degrees within Taurus.

[Fol. 2 *a*]

5. *Almayrem* - fifth unfortunate mansion, the red unfortunate face of Moon. When the Moon descends in it, make all of the images of joining [and] of friendship and you will have a good fortune. It will start in the end of the fourth [mansion] and cross into the Twins[4], [that is, the] end of Taurus and the head of Gemini.

6. *Altihiakh* - face of Mars and red fortune. When the Moon was in it, make the images of peace and love. It starts at the end of the fifth and is limited to seventeen degrees within Gemini, and it is the belly of Gemini.

[S h-L page 8]

7. *Adunto* - face of Jupiter, fortunate, mixed red and white. When the Moon was in it, the images of beasts and the field animals [for operations] of the peace, love, and any good should be made. It starts at the end of Virgo[5] and is limited to the end of Gemini.

8. *Anterakh* - red and white fortune face of Mars. When the Moon is in it, make the images of water, the sea, and rivers. It starts at the head of

---

[1] The word "love" here and throughout this translation is used as the equivalent of the Middle to Early Modern English "dilection," which appears in the corresponding sections of *Liber Lunæ*.

[2] This is understood to mean that the second mansion starts at 12° Aries and ends at 26° Aries.

[3] "(mg. fire)" = the word "fire" is written in the margin (Latin: *margen* = *mg.*) at this place.

[4] "The Twins" – in *Sepher ha-Levanah* this is given as *te'umim*, namely Gemini.

[5] "Virgo" here should read "Gemini."

Cancer and is limited to twelve degrees within it.

9. *Aaorat* - white fortune face of the Sun. Make there the images of all fowls. It starts at the end of the eighth and is limited to twenty five degrees of Cancer, [within] the body of the Cancer.

10. *Algiarekh* - white fortune face of Venus. When the Moon descends in it, make images of wolves, foxes, and all beasts. It starts at the end of the ninth and is limited to eight degrees within Leo. And it is the end of Cancer and the head of Leo.

11. *Ararab* - black fortune face of Mercury. When the Moon was in it, make images of loss, destruction, binding, fornication, and separation. It starts at the end of the tenth and is limited to twenty-one degrees within Leo, and it is the body of Leo.

12. *Azada* - white fortune face of Moon. When the Moon descends in it, make the images of love, society, and any good. It starts at the end of the eleventh and is limited to four degrees within Virgo. End of Leo and head of Virgo.

[S h-L page 9]

13. *Alanq* - white fortune face of Saturn. When the Moon descends in it, make images of love and everything you will ever desire to attain. It starts at the end of the twelfth and is limited to seventeen degrees within Virgo, the belly of Virgo.

14. *Akamekh* - white and red fortune [of] Mercury and [it] is the chosen[1] face of Jupiter. When the Moon descends in it, make images of alliance, inclination, every friendship and love. It starts at the end of the thirteenth and is limited within the last degree of Virgo, [the] end of Virgo.

15. *Algrasheim* - white fortune face of Mars. When the Moon descends in it, make images of adversity and evil to whatever you will desire. It starts at the end of the fourteenth and is limited to twelve degrees in Libra.

---

[1] "Chosen" here means *most beneficial, most favorable,* or *most profitable,* like *select* when used as an adjective.

16. *Anheni* - bad fortune face of the Sun. When the Moon is in it, make images of destruction, desolation, and binding. It starts at the end of the fifteenth and is limited to twenty five degrees in Libra, the belly of Libra.

17. *Alikil* - bad fortune face of Venus. When the Moon is in it, make images of discord and any evil. It starts at the end of the sixteenth and is limited to eight degrees within Scorpio, the end of Libra and the head of Scorpio.

[Fol. 2 *b*]

18. *Ashibarekh* - the heart of Scorpio and white fortune face of Mercury. When the Moon descends in it, make images of any good, the binding of the tongues, and silence. It starts at the end of the seventeenth and is limited to twenty one degrees within Scorpio.

[S h-L page 10]

19. *Alqalab* - bad fortune face of Moon. When the Moon is in it, make images of fornication, discord, and binding of the will. It starts at the end of the eighteenth and is limited to the fourth degree within Sagittarius, [the] beginning of Sagittarius and the end of Scorpio.

20. *Anami* - white fortune face of Saturn. When the Moon is in it, make images for the arousal of peace, love, and friendship. It starts at the end of the nineteenth and is limited to seventeen degrees within Sagittarius, the belly of Sagittarius.

21. *Shalberakh* - good fortune face of Jupiter. When the Moon is in it, make images of cooperation and silence. It starts at the end of the twentieth and is limited to the last degree[s] within Sagittarius, the end of Sagittarius.

22. *Shdadebed* - bad fortune face of Mars. When the Moon is in it, make images of evil. It starts at the beginning of Capricorn and is limited to twelve degrees within it, the belly of Capricorn.

23. *Shadbula* - good fortune face of Sun. When the Moon is in it, make images of any good. It starts at the end of the twenty-second and is limited to twenty-five degrees, [the] end of Capricorn and the head of Aquarius. And it will be interpreted as the fortune of fortunes.

24. *Shadplatokh* - good fortune face of Venus. When the Moon is in it,

make images of any good. It starts at the end of the twenty-third and is limited to eight degrees within Aquarius.

[S h-L page 11]

25. *Shadligiakh* - face of Mercury white fortune. When the Moon is in it, make images of silence and binding. It starts at the end of the twenty-fourth and is limited to twenty one degrees within Aquarius, the belly of Aquarius.

26. *Algrash* - good fortune face of Moon. When the Moon is in it, make images of alliance, cooperation, and friendship. It starts at the end of the twenty-fifth and is limited to four degrees within Pisces. [The] end of Aquarius and [the] head of Pisces.

27. *Alprag* - the last bad [mansion] and red fortune face of Saturn. When the Moon descends in it, make images of separation, binding, and every infirmity. It starts at the end of the twenty-sixth and is limited to seven degrees within Pisces, the belly of Pisces.

28. *Albetan* - white fortune face of Jupiter. When the Moon descends in it, make images of any good that you will desire, and any matter that will go directly before governors by you, it will be completed by the commandment of the Creator, blessed be He. It starts at the end of the twenty-seventh and is limited to the last degree[s] within Pisces, [the] end of Pisces.

(3) **On Potions**[1]

Here are the potions with which all images of good, alliance, and friendship will be suffumed. They are wood: *Alvay, Albimum, Shperam, Piluzas,* which means to say *Atzer*. From each of them a fourth part will be taken and will be used, or *Haload* - which is to say good wood...[2]

[S h-L page 12]
Azomeri - which means to say wood *Mzimeria* and it is [from] an island in the countries *Handia, Vezapran, Pilozosh* and *Azen*. A quarter of ounce from each of them.[3]

[Fol. 3 a]

The potions with which images of evil, discord, and separation will be suffumed are *Almashakh, Alapor, Atzbrala, Shoer, Triataneral,* and *Alidanam*. From each of them a fourth part of an ounce will be taken, and every one will use *Alnazaq, Alzipar. Azekra, Lazoeti. Shriado, Shaltziya, Shandal, Aldinar, Aloesh* black.[4]

[5]**Said** the philosopher *Kelenus* that first, God, blessed be He, you need the names of the hours of the day and night, because one is committed to pray using them for assistance through their force in nature and their strength by the commandment of the Creator, blessed be He.

---

[1] This title could be translated 'Of Drugs' or 'About Poisons,' or more likely 'Of Potions.' The corresponding passage in *Liber Lunæ* § 2 (86v-87r) indicates 'suffumigations.'

[2] The varieties of wood which we might discern here are oak, sandalwood, and aloes.

[3] 'Azomeri' and 'Mzimeria' refer to 'marine wood,' namely *wood from an island*, possibly *driftwood*. The corresponding passage in *Liber Lunæ* (*fol.* 86v) reads

> Suffumigacions of worchings of love and of reflexion and of all good these be the names Aload alkumeri – i – signu de Amnaria wich is some Iland in the parties of India Azafran.

'Vezapran,' *Liber Lunæ's* 'Azafran,' is Arabic for *saffron*.

[4] Missing at this place is mention of the 54 or 55 angels and their names. This appears to have been displaced to § (1), the last paragraph.

[5] The section beginning here through the cycle of the hours of the day resembles Sloane MS 3826 *fols*. 78r-78v more closely than it does the corresponding section of *Liber Lunæ*.

Know that the **first hour** of any day will be called *Yubitum*, or *Yebean* in another version. And at that hour humans will pray in front of their Creator, and this is the hour of binding the tongues of every human being.

The second hour will be called *Geornorim, or Genorim* in another version. At that hour the angels will pray in front of their Creator. And images of friendship, and peace among all of the creatures and human beings, and the joining of their minds or spirits in another version, will be made.

The third hour will be called *Banur*, or *Rampur* in another version. At this hour the fowls will thank their Creator. And image of fish and of all fowls - which means to say pigeons (the progeny of pigeons) – will be made.

[S h-L page 13]

The fourth hour will be called *Tzelbim*, or *Tzel Gehim* in another version. At that hour creatures will [give] thanks to their Creator, and images of serpents and scorpions will be made.

The fifth hour will be called *Tzealekh*, or *Tzlalekh* in another version. At that hour all of the beasts which were created will [give] thanks to their Creator, and images of beasts and wolves will be made.

The sixth hour will be called *Tzidamhor*, or *Tehmor* in another version. At that hour *Kerubay*[1] will pray because of the sins of humans. Images of captivity and freedom will be made.

The seventh hour will be called *Yador*. At that hour the angels who bear the throne will pray, and images of peace between kings and ministers will be made.

The eighth hour will be called *Yaporim*, or *Yapoim* in another version. At that hour images of separation and discord among humans will be made.

The ninth hour will be called *Ra*, or *Baron* in another version. At that hour images of people who travel on the roads and who want to be saved from impediments and exploiters, so [that these] will never rise against him, will be made.

---

[1] *Kerubim*, the order of angels.

The tenth hour will be called *Yahim*, or *Yakhon* in another version. At that hour water will sing to its Creator so that the spirit of God will descend on it when its eyes are raised. Images of the imprisonment of kings and ministers will be made and God will enter them so that they will not speak badly to him at the hour when they are with him.

[S h-L page 14]

The eleventh hour will be called *Yebrim*, or *Yehrim* in another version. At that hour the righteous will have joy, and images of friendship, love, and peace will be made.

The twelfth hour will be called *Rayalom* or *Rayalon* in another version. At that hour images of silence will be made so that they will never talk those for whom you will make this operation.

(4) The names of the hours of the night and their images.

And these are more powerful and are more highly praised than the images which are made in the day.[1]

The first hour of any night will be called *Amen*, or *Hanem* in another version. At that hour the demons' prayers to their Creator will be made. Then, no one will give rise to any impediment to anyone else until they return from their prayer. At that hour images of silence will be made.

The second hour will be called *Thmbeyi*, or *Tibezimer* in another version. At that hour fish will sing to their Creator and all of the beasts which are in the water and the reptiles which are on earth [will sing as well]. At that hour images of fish, leeches, frogs, and all of the beasts which are in the water will be made so that they won't move from their place.

The third hour will be called *Thathor*, or *Dahor* in another version. At that hour the beasts will sing to their Creator. At that hour images of fire will be made so that they will not burn. And images of serpents and poisonous snakes will be made so that they won't cause any harm. And at that hour, humans will be bound in order not to speak.

[S h-L page 15]

The fourth hour will be called *Alahir*. At that hour demons will hover over graves. An impediment will occur if a person who is frightened is found there, and whose hair will stand on end like an ostrich and [show] horror. At that hour images will be made and will be engraved from gold to peace and the passionate love, and this is the image of those hovering.

The fifth hour will be called *Kamaypur*. At that hour the water will rest and sing to its Creator. At that hour images of clouds and uncanny storms will be made.

The sixth hour will be called *Razom*, or *Zarori* in another version. At that hour the waters will rest and will also stay calm[2] even if it is stormy. And if at that very hour the water is anointed by someone who is involved in

---

[1] This section corresponds to *Liber Lunæ fols.* 90r-92v, but more closely resembles Sloane MS 3826 *fols.* 78v-80r.

[2] "Stay calm" – alternatively "stagnate"

anointing of those who have fevers and could not sleep, the sleep will be brought back to them and they will rest by the commandment of the Creator to be blessed. At that hour images of visions [will be made] by which anything one can see which is proper to do in the world as a vision will be done.

The seventh hour will be called *Yapor*, or *Yaper* in another version. At that hour images of kings and ministers will be made. If someone asks something from them, he will attain it and [they] will never turn him down.

The eighth hour will be called *Zimali*. At that hour the land-seeds will give thanks to their Creator. At that hour images of gardens, orchards, trees, and all of the land-seeds will be made so that they will have good fortune and will be preserved from any harm, by the wish of the Creator, blessed be He.

The ninth hour will be called *Tzepar*, or *Zeparim* in another version. At that hour the angels will pray to God to bind the world. At that hour images will be made in front of kings and ministers in order to bind issues of humans' wishes and all of the creatures, and to repel their harm.

[S h-L page 16]

The tenth hour will be called *Nahalqo*, or *Malko* in another version, and it is a great benefit. At that hour images which prevent all of the women of the country from fornication or [prevent] any particular woman [from fornication] will be made.

The eleventh hour will be called *Alako*, or *Alatho* in another version. At that hour the gates of heaven will be opened. When the human calls to his Creator, all of his wishes will be fulfilled by his belief. At that hour, images of peace, strength, love which will never be removed, and courtship will be made. And that hour will also be called *Indino*, as it is [called] all over the country. And at that hour the Sun will pray to the creatures of the supreme Creator from its holy residence.

The twelfth hour will be called *Shelem*, or *Shellem* in another version. At that hour the host of heaven will take a rest until the humans pray to their supreme Creator. At that hour images of silence and letting will be made and [it] will be called the image of horror and fear. The one who will look [Fol. 4 a] at it [the image] will be frightened and shiver like an ignoramus and he will not have the ability to speak. And everything that will be done at that hour will never be removed by anyone, and it is confirmed. The images indeed will be made from four kinds of metal: tin, gold, brass, and silver.

(5) **Aspects[1] of the Sun-Signs.**

Each Sun-sign will be divided to three equal parts, and each part has within [it] ten degrees and [it] will be called a *face*. And if you know the degree

[S h-L page 17]

which grows within them, you should observe what hour it is and the degree [to] which its fortune is dark. Fifteen degrees are growing.

Picture of   Saturn * * Jupiter * * Mars
Sun * * Venus * * Mercury * * Moon. * *   [See plate 1: *opposite title page*]

The growing face when on the first day or in the beginning of the day, the Sun-sign will enter and it is joined to the scepter of the Sun. When the Sun and the Moon are in one Sun-sign, the joining is called *growing fortune* or *the growing of the fortune* - which is to say *fortuna*.

---

[1] "Aspects" could be rendered "Faces."

(6) **The Images of the Day**[1]

[The First Image]

Said *Kelinos* that the first image will be made in the first hour of any day in order to bind tongues so that they will never speak ill. Here, the image which is half silver and half tin will be fused, and the Moon being in any of its four quarters,[2] be made on a human figure. And at the first hour of the day, the name of the lord of the image will be engraved on its [the image's] head. On that day the name of the first hour will be engraved on its breast. And the names *Bilakh* and *Rilakh* will be engraved on its abdomen, and [you will] bury it in the entrance. And that image, which is bound [as described], is confirmed by all tongues, eyes, and hearts. Write the names of the Sun [and] the Moon, and the name of the angel of the time [or year] in which it the image will be made, on its breast. And bury it and write on the ridge [rim] from the image the precious names by which the Creator, blessed be He, created the heaven, earth, sea, and everything which is in them.

[S h-L page 18]

And firmly write the names in order to restrain and bind the tongues [to obtain what you will] from whomever you desire among humans, the rest of the beasts, and the fowls. And carve [the names of] its angels on each of them. And these are the names that you will engrave, and if you also read them toward whatever you desire to repel, it will be repelled; and you will read them in reverse order: *Lamitrorosh, Lalakim, Lanporish, Langbali, Lashepim, Wel, Lashepet.* Regarding these names, their operation, one way or the other, will bind anything one will ever desire, or prevent what you [do not] desire, and to unbind with them by themselves. Truly, if one intends to make the image of binding and restraining, these names will be read first in the correct order while the image is being engraved. All the same, if one intends to make the images of expulsion, the names will be read in reverse order so that the intended operation will not be in vain, and these names are [to be] hidden from all. It is true that you should be careful when you complete the

---

[1] This section of *Sepher ha-Levanah* expands on § (3), ¶ 4 *ff.*, after the two paragraphs on "potions." This parallels *Liber Lunæ fols.* 87r-89v. *Liber Lunæ* tacks on the names of the hours at the end of each section; these names are similar to those in *Sepher ha-Levanah* § (3).

[2] "Four phases," i.e., of the Moon. This is my surmise for the meaning of the letter *dalet*, which in Hebrew is also used to indicate '4.' Otherwise the words "the Moon *dalet*'" in the text interrupt the flow of the sentence.. Without this phrase, the clause reads, "it will be made on a human figure." The alternative, but less likely choice of "being in any of the four quarters" is based on the equivalent passage in *Liber Lunæ fol.* 87r.

operation of an image when you say the thing that you desire to bind at the same time as the names of the image are engraved. Whether it is a village, or a town, or a city, or country, or authority, or the mating of man, woman, beasts, animals, fowls, clouds and winds. In general, everything that you bind or desire to prevent according to what has [been] mentioned, you will read the names themselves and you will have a good fortune.

The Second Image

will be made in the second hour of any day and it will be called the image of alliance and real peace. The image will be made of silver and tin with heads (it seems to be chert[1]) which are being fused. At that hour, the names of their lords will be engraved on their heads. The name of the lord of the hour will be engraved on their breasts, and the names that will be engraved on their abdomens are the following: *Bahalim, …*

[S h-L page 19]

Madualim, Manopiqon, Priolam, Nalkatan, Berharim. And when the two images, which were mentioned, are made, [these] things will be engraved on their breasts with fine wax. Then, place each one of them in a house – which is to say the man and the woman in whom you have desired to rouse their love in a way that others will pass over them, and their love will never be broken.

The Third Image

[Fol. 4 *b*.]

will be made in the third hour of any day and will be called the image of binding all fish and fowls. Here, the image will be made of which fish or fowl that you desire [to restrain], and the names of the angels of the hour will be engraved on its abdomen. Then, it will be suffumed with green aloes and red sandalwood and it will be buried in that very place for which it was made. If the image of a fish is made, it will be buried in the water. And one will see the wonderful things from this work of the things that are being heard to that very thing itself by the commandment of the Creator, blessed be He.

The Fourth Image

will be made in the fourth hour of any day and will be called the image of scorpions, serpents, poisonous snakes, and all harmful reptiles. And it will be called the image of different beasts. Here, it will be made at the above-

---

[1] *Chert*, namely, quartz, agate, chalcedony, jasper, or flint.

mentioned hour, and write the name of the beast which you desire to bind on its head. And the name of the angel of the hour on its abdomen, and the precious names of the first hour will be written on its breast. And it will be buried in the area where the beasts of that species reside and from them [the beasts] the image was made. And as long as that image is there, that species of beasts cannot depart.

[S h-L page 20]

The Fifth Image

will be made in the fifth hour of any day and will be called the image of wolves, hares, and the rest of the beasts which are similar to these. And it will be made of silver on [which there is] a picture of the beast that you have desired to bind. And the name of the beast and the name of the lord of the hour will be engraved on its breast, and the names of the first hour [will be engraved] on its abdomen. And it will be suffumed with aloes and red sandalwood and will be buried in an area on the other side of that species of beasts, and one will have a good fortune.

The Sixth Image

will be made in the sixth hour of any day and will be called the image of prisoners and captives. And it will be made in the shape of man or woman and it will be made of either tin or silver. And one will write the name of the man or the woman on its head, and [you] will write the name of the lord of the hour on its breast, and the name of the first hour on its abdomen and it will be suffumed. Then, it will be given to the man or woman for whom it was made, and he/she will be released on that day. Likewise, it will be made to bind water which you will desire to bind it, and you will have good fortune with the assistance of the Creator, blessed be He.

The Seventh Image

will be made in the seventh hour of any day. It is useful when entering before ministers and kings and one will attain passionate love and great admiration.

[S h-L page 21]

And the image will be made of silver, and the name of the king will be engraved on its head. Likewise, the names of the first hour [will be engraved] on its abdomen. And when one enters in front of the king, he will carry the image with him and will attain anything he desires by the wish of the Creator.

The Eighth Image

will be made in the eighth hour of any day and will be called the image of desolation and the expulsion of humans that they will not stand inside a house or a compartment during any [such] operation. And the image will be made of red brass with two heads the first of is a human head and the second is a donkey head. And write the name of either the nation or the person or the [person's family] on its head, and write the name of the lord of the hour on its breast, and the names of the first hour on its abdomen. And you will suffume it with human blood of a slain person and his fat. And bury it where you desire to repel the people for whom the image was made, and you will see from it wonderful things by the commandment of the Creator, blessed be He.

The Ninth Image

[Fol. 5 a.]

will be made in the ninth hour of any day in order to bind thieves. And a human image will be made of silver, and write its name on its head, and the names of the angels of darkness on its breast, and the name of the first hour on its abdomen. And suffume it with clean aloes and crocus, and carry it with you so that thieves will be frightened and become addled. And you will be saved from them by the commandment of the Creator, blessed be He.

[S h-L page 22]

The Tenth Image

will be made in the tenth hour of any day. This is the image of alliance and friendship between two people who hate each other. And two images will be made in the eleventh hour, and they are made of either the finest silver or of tin with the same weight [or value]. And write their names on their heads, and the name of the lord of the hour on their breasts, and the name of the first hour on their abdomens. And suffume them with clean aloes and crocus, and join them together and bury them in a low fire. And one will come to you with open arms wherever you desire.

The Eleventh Image

will be made in the eleventh hour of any day to tighten, maintain, and give rise to love and friendship of all human beings. The image will be made of silver. Write its name on its head and the name of the lord of the hour on its breast, and write the names of the angels of love and binding on its abdomen. Suffume it with white aloes and crocus and carry it with you in a white silk cloth and you will attain anything that you will desire.

The Twelfth Image

will be made in the twelfth hour of any day to bind tongues. Make the image from tin in any shape that you desire and carve its name on its head, and the name of the lord of the hour on its breast, and the names of the first hour and the binding on its abdomen. And suffume it with clean aloes wood and crocus.

[S h-L page 23]

Then, bury it below the threshold until the thing which you desire will pass over it. Then, put it in a white silk cloth and carry it with you. And write on the ridge [rim] from the image of horror:[1] *and these are the names which are hidden by the wise men.* Then, suffume it, and before you bury it, you should recite this oath: *I will swear by the words of the holies and by the holy name that in their [the words'] power, you will burn them.*

And you should call each of them by his name: *Shamliel, Shaniul, Ansharosh, Arish, Taliq, Umailra, Maiil, Abra, Shuash, Abarhi, Labransh, Hatzion, Mamor, Vetuparon, Apnatam, Manshie, Harqod, El, Ayishtail, Aayabiril, Beliyar, Veter, El, Abray, Aair, Durquminat, Venash, Shiar, Mirar, Atuamkan, Sheabshaush, Shopa or Kilash.* Then, you should suffume it with *Malo, Azaraq,* and *Znedresh* below the seventh array of wood for the sacrifices set to any night when you say the names over it.

---

[1] Above, in *Sepher ha-Levanah* § (4), the word and idea of *horror* appear in the passage on the fourth hour of the night, and the "image of horror" is mentioned in the passage on the twelfth hour of the night.

The Images of the Night[1]

The First Image will be made in the first hour of any night. As in the tale of the bathhouses and silence, said *Kelinos*, When someone asks another to make for him a bath, etc., you should take iron or fused brass and make a candelabra – which is to say a vessel which has seven mouths – and write

[Fol. 5 b.]

on each of the mouths the following names: *Tzpratzetin, Shetzeshin, Haypashin, Barhin, Dalin, Shshhin*. And on every mouth there is one wick which is covered with oil. And you should write on the underside of the vessel, these being the hidden words which are from [the image of] horror: *Nurin, Baldekin, Zahir, Yapunin, Alkar, Badikin, Anadin, Shnikin*.

(Beginning of plate 6a)

[S h-L page 24]

And make on the above-mentioned vessel an image which is made of brass in a shape of a man who holds either a brass candle or an oil jug in his hand, as if he were pouring oil without turning the vessel over. And write on the face of the image the two following names: *Ramerail, Laudpil*, also on its abdomen, and on the underside of the vessel ([the] signs of *Mars* and *Saturn*[2]). And either seal it or bury its face so that it will never be revealed.

The Second Image

will be made to prevent fornication. Said *Kelinos*, When I entered the city, which is called *Laidar*, I recovered an image so that a woman will never fornicate there. Then, God, blessed be He, make the image from clean brass and write on it the following names: *Pelblakh, Hormorsh, Rayshank, Shiqolim, Zuzanur, Kaminakh*, and write the other following names on a brass tray and put the tray in the hand of the image to carry it: *Zakino, Zelmani, Shorabim, Inukiel* or *Mukiel, Nukiun, Shushniun, Eka*. Then, the image will be buried in either the city, or the village, or the house which you will desire, and it will be completed by the commandment of the Creator, blessed be He. Also, you can perform [an operation] to fish, frogs, and every reptile in the world.

---

[1] This section parallels *Liber Lunæ fols.* 90r-92v.
[2] In the text, the symbols of Mars and Saturn are shown instead of words.

The Third Image

will be made in the third hour of any night to repel any harmful beast such as serpents, scorpions, dogs, mice, and similar beasts. The image will be made of brass of any beast that you desire [to repel].

[S h-L page 25]

And write on its face the following names either on the border of the area or in a passage of three ways, or any compartment that you will desire. And no beast which looks like the shape of the image will remain there: *Ventroton*, or *Obatron* in another version. *Boriun*, or *Barayon* in another version. *Proshimion, Papraril, Roboton.*

The Fourth Image

will be made in the fourth hour of any night to destroy either houses, or villages, or towns, and to reverse any transaction or the endeavors of your enemies. Take urine from a camel and write on the entrance of your enemy, *Kulintheosh, Ziniqit, Pergul, Tzidorion, Gintayan*, and you should say, *I will swear you in so that you will lose either the house, the business, or the thing* [say the name of that which is to be lost or destroyed] *which belongs to someone* [say the name of the owner of said property], and it will be.

The Fifth Image

will be made in the fifth hour of any night to release a host of clouds or hail and give rise to discord among human beings. Two images will be made: one will be made of lead and the other will be made of red brass of the same weight, namely, 65 drams [each]. And engrave on them the following characters:

And suffume them and say over them the names of the angels, and bury them in a high place in either city, or village, or a house, and hatred or discord will befall between them: *Tzithum, Pebil, Olakon.* All the same, if you desire to release clouds and repel beasts as you will desire, you should bury them in the highest place of either the city, or the yard, or the house, and it will be completed by the desire of the Creator, blessed be He. [End of plate 6a]

The Sixth Image

will be made in the sixth hour of any night and it will be made of red brass and will be called the image of repulsion and expulsion. And the names of the angles of repulsion and expulsion will be engraved on it, and they [the names] are: *Belian, Raki, E, Aolim, Abrakim, Apolenu, Hadaliom* or *Hentinavivi*. And write on its forehead the name [of him] that you desire to expel from a house or a city, and bury the image in the above-mentioned area.

The Seventh Image

will be made in the seventh hour of any night to burn grapevines, trees, and other kinds of greenery. Make the image from red brass and carve on it the following names, and bury it in the border of the compartment, and it will burn the privately owned land as far as ten miles: *Ayar, Katinath, Hanranan, Kabed, Hubrah, Hayad, Mathayad, Maurathi, Kaprea, Adetzir, Mare –* which is to say, Heavenly fire will burn a fire in honor of the Creator, blessed be He, as the fire of *Abligelil*.

$$\text{lo} \, x \, \text{cb} \, 3 \, \text{boeb} \, 2 \, \text{cb} \, \text{pbi} \, \text{h}$$

Burn by the wish of the Creator, blessed be He.

The Eighth Image

will be made in the eighth hour of any night to join together fowls and the progeny of pigeons which are [within] ten miles around you, until you hunt them. The image will be made of any shape of any fowl that you desire, and will be made of the finest gold. Its weight is one *mina*. (*mg*: not certain)[1]

And engrave on them the following names: *Yardak, Rathinakh, Adokh, Akilokh*. The fowls [will] come here from everywhere; Gabriel will remove you [fowls] from [within] any side of the ten miles. And bury it in the highest place either in a city or a village and the fowls will be gathered around it. And on the face [of the image] you can make any bird which you desire to join together and to gather by the wish of the Creator, blessed be He.

---

[1] A *mina* was a unit of weight (and currency) equal to about 1.25 lbs (or 0.57 kg). (*mg*: not certain) = in the margin (= *mg.*) here is written "not certain."

The Ninth Image

will be made in the ninth hour of any night to gather all of the fowls from any one of the hills which you desire. The image will be made showing any fowl that you desire, and it will be made of one ounce of gold and it will be hollow. And carve on it the names which are below, and bury it in the highest place there. And every one of that same species will be gathered [from] ten miles around. And these are the names:

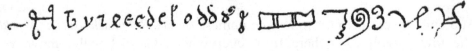

Shur, Bnishor, Mukal, Mokiel, Viviniesh, Rel, Ba.

The Tenth Image

will be made in the tenth hour of any night to separate those [who are] beloved [of themselves][1] so that peace will never be between them. The image will be made of tin and the fourth part will made of red brass with its length being one little finger – which is to say one palm. Then, make another image which is similar to the former and write on each of them the names that are of them [for whom] you made those images. And write on the breast the names of the angels of separation and write on the ridge [rim] the names which you will see [below].

[S h-L page 28]

Then, you suffume them and separately bury each of them in different places so that they will never join together. Also, in this way you can give rise to any discord that you desire between them.

[End of plate 6b] [Fol. 6 *b*]

---

[1] The additions in brackets are based on *Liber Lunæ* 92r: "them that loveth them self"

The Eleventh Image

will be made in the eleventh hour of any night to bring or remove a man or a woman from any area where you desire. The image will be made of one ounce of silver or tin, making what is depicted as pretty as is possible. And engrave its name on its head the name of the eleventh hour [and engrave] on its breast [the name] which is *Geberum*. And write the following precious names on its abdomen: *Arogion, Ranial, Bebeni, Itzekalish, Leshmelim, Raran, Larmnaim, Giriqalon, Lebar, Delalion, Pimaron, Shviaday, Melon*. Then, bury it in a low fire and [it will] bring that woman to you at the same night that you will command [her].

The Twelfth Image

will be made in the twelfth hour of any night to twist the face and quake the body. The image will be made of red brass on any figure that you desire. And the face will be opposite to its ridge [rim], and its feet will be opposite to its hands and its hands [will be] where the feet should be. And write its name on its head, and the names of horror on its back, and bury it in the entrance of his house and his body will be frightened and will tremble and [he] will become insane as long as the image will be turned upside down.

[S h-L page 29]

Or put it under a tree *Alkayneye*, or *Alkamed* in another version, and his suffering will be upon the eleventh hour. And these are the names: *Adpago, Hum, Alin, Avag, Maad, Shadah. Qaralash, Malash, Mahah, Thuarum, Thala, Dobilin*.

The images of the day and night were completed.

The tale of the images by *Petolmeo*[1] is truer and rarer with its experience than the other versions which merely brushed the surface of the images of the zodiac. *Alborakeq* said, When the Eastern people make those images, they will not pay attention to others. They will only be careful that the growing will be *karshtropa* when they operate and then they will have a good fortune.

Done and Completed

Praise to God

Creator of the World.

---

[1] Ptolemy

SUPPLEMENTARY MATERIAL

THE TWENTY-EIGHT MANSION OF THE MOON:

a paraphrase in contemporary English combining
Liber Lunæ fols. 84-86v and *Sepher ha-Levanah* §§ 1 and 2 [Fols. 1 *b*-2 *b*][1]

[84] Hermes said: I have studied all the books on all of the planets, but I have never seen one truer or more perfect than this most precious book named *Liber Lunæ*. But first, before God I witness, I admonish you to hide it from all men or else on the Day of Judgment God will inquire of you what was done by it, for by this book both good and evil may be done, in any month and on any day that one wishes. It is a most precious and secret book, for it contains the ineffable name of God by which [84v] He carries out all works, both good and evil, for He by His name implements both righteous and unrighteous deeds. Therefore, hold fast to what I have written, fear God, and beware that you not show this book to anyone, for if anyone else touches it, it will become polluted. Do not let anyone else perform the operations and purifications in this book. If you steer away from all impurity, the work done by this book will be magnified and your desires will be fulfilled.

When you want to make a talismanic image by this book, recite over it the names of the angels serving the cycle of the Moon. Suffume it seven times with precious aromatics and suffumigations. Recite over it seven times the names of the work by which you will perform the operation, and recite the name of the hour, the name of Luna, the name of the mansion in which Luna resides, and the name of the day on which the operation is performed. And if the mansion of the operation holds a rulership or exaltation, there will be a hastening of the work, with the help of God.

[2]These are the names of the angels who serve the images of the Moon through its cycle over which you must swear seven times with each suffumigation. These are the names of the angels whose secrets shall improve your understanding and increase your wisdom. You must keep these names hidden:

---

[1] Numbers in brackets indicate folio pages from *Liber Lunæ*.
[2] This paragraph follows in *Sepher ha-Levanah* [Fol. 1 *b*].

Comeil Cemeil Charochin azardin reanei abras achithim abrancasai larabusin Iangas angarozan mamenim hacsemim mimgogm labelas mezetin farbarakin candanegin iaciz andonin rasaidin saphianim barthaylin aninei Neilin borcolin balkanaritin arieisin abranorin cannamdin andalasin carnnamdin sarajemin Adiamenim soe saeosin Jachehay feresin deibenim mediesin heizamamin Janozothin Abramathin bifulica begehalodin gaforin azafirin barionin matnairelin genira manderilin.[1]

[2]Bolemus said: The mansion of *Meliatalh*, the first mansion, which is the face of Mars, is an evil mansion. It starts at the beginning of Aries and concludes at twelve-and-a-half degrees Aries. Within the influence of this mansion, you should recite the names of its cycle. In this mansion make images of separation, discord, and hatred.

Albutaim, the second mansion, which is the *belly of Aries*[3], is a fortunate mansion. It starts at twelve degrees Aries and concludes at twenty-six degrees Aries. When Luna descends in this mansion, make images of all things to be bound and joined together, namely, images of hope, love and friendship.

[4]*Aqhoranay*, or *Alturayib* in another version, the third mansion at the end of Aries and the head of Taurus, is the white face, or fortunate aspect, of Venus. It begins at the end of the second mansion and concludes at eight degrees Taurus. When the Moon is in this mansion, make images of words of grace and make images of the things which you desire to join together.

Aldeboran, the fourth mansion, which is the eye of Taurus, is the evil face of Mercury. It begins at the end of the third mansion and concludes at twenty-one degrees Taurus. When Luna [85] descends in this mansion, make images of adversity, desolation, loss, and evil.

---

[1] The names here are from *Liber Lunæ fols.* 86v-87.

    Sepher ha-Levanah § 1 gives the following names: *Anailim, Quntzilim, Gashgorzim, Aqashimadi, Amikhilim, Abrakiim, Abrashim, Lairayozim, Yamaghash, Manenim, Mangororam, Hartninay, Montaginim, Latzandonim, Qamshilindim, Shaamam, Sharailim, Amaamilim, Haqoilim, Balknaritim, Arihaylim, Beqshdeilim, Abranodomilim, Qarmayndim, Andalashim, Sharahitzinim, Adiamenim, Tzetahotim, Yatzarpnishim, Teibinenim, Nehelim. Hiraminim, Abramatim, Lanagotim, Wipoliyaqa, Belgahalidim, Gaporim, Aqrapirim, Tayriomim, Diqomeylim, Genithokim, Madarilim, Kearldim, Yebrunkhelim, Aladim, Yadalim, Shethakam, Panaplor, Badaylin, Dabnotirorin.*

[2] *Liber Lunæ fol.* 84v continues here.

[3] The Arabic name for the second mansion, *al butain*, means "belly [of Aries]."

[4] This paragraph is entirely derived from *Sepher ha-Levanah*; *Liber Lunæ* omits the third mansion.

Almaycen, the fifth mansion, is the evil red face of Luna. It starts at the end of the fourth mansion and concludes in the head of Gemini. When Luna descends in this mansion, make images of adversity and allegation, or make images of building. If you make images of alliance and friendship, you will have good fortune.

Althaya, the sixth mansion, is the fortunate red face of Saturn.[1] It starts at the end of the fifth mansion and concludes at seventeen degrees Gemini. When Luna descends in this mansion, make images of whatever you wish to be fulfilled by the workings of God, and, accordingly, make images of peace and love.

Addiraen, the seventh mansion at the end of Gemini, is interpreted *Brachia*. It is the fortunate face of Jupiter, mixed white and red. It starts at the end of the sixth mansion and concludes at the end of Gemini. When Luna descends in it, make images of wild beasts, concord and love, and all good things. Make images of beasts and field animals for operations of love and peace.

Innatar, the eighth mansion at the head of Cancer, is the fortunate red and white face of Mars. It starts at the beginning of Cancer and concludes at twelve degrees Cancer. When Luna descends in it, make images of water, i.e., the sea, rivers, etc., of ships, and of floods.

Alkaud, the ninth mansion in the womb of Cancer, is interpreted *highness*. It is the fortunate white face of the Sun. It starts at the end of the eighth mansion and concludes at twenty-five degrees Cancer. In this mansion, make images of fowls, big and small, and of pigeons, and thereby you will profit.

Algeibh, the tenth mansion at the end of Cancer and the beginning of Leo, is interpreted the *front of him*.[2] It is the fortunate white face of Venus. It starts at the end of the ninth mansion and concludes at eight degrees Leo. In this mansion make images of wolves, foxes, and wild beasts.

Azobra, the eleventh mansion in the heart of Leo, which is also called *Azumble*, is the evil black face of Mercury. It starts at the end of the eleventh mansion and concludes at twenty-one degrees Leo. When Luna descends in this mansion, make images of destruction, fornication, separation, and allegation, or of binding and infirmity — or of distinction, and thereby you will profit.

---

[1] *Sepher ha-Levanah* has "face of Mars and red fortune"
[2] *Front of him* – i.e., the lion's "forehead," *al jabhah*, which is the name of the tenth mansion in Arabic.

Algapha, the twelfth mansion, the tail of Leo and the head of Virgo, is the fortunate white face [85v] of Luna. It starts at the end of the eleventh mansion and concludes at four degrees Virgo. When Luna descends in it, make images of love, friendship, society, and of all things that you would build.

Alans, the thirteenth mansion, the womb of Virgo, is the fortunate white face of Saturn. It starts at the end of the twelfth mansion and concludes at seventeen degrees Virgo. When Luna descends in this mansion, make images of love and of anything that you would shape and join together.

Alchumech, the fourteenth mansion at the end of Virgo, is red face of Jupiter, the most profitable and fortunate face.[1] It starts at the end of the thirteenth and concludes at the last degree of Virgo. When Luna descends in this mansion, make images of alliance, love, and friendship.

Algarst, the fifteenth mansion at the head of Libra, is the evil red face of Mars.[2] It starts at the end of the fourteenth mansion and concludes at twelve degrees Libra. In this mansion, make images of evil and tribulation, and the destruction of whatever you wish to hinder.

Azubene, the sixteenth mansion in the middle of Libra, is the evil face of the Sun. It starts at the end of the fifteenth mansion and concludes at twenty-five degrees Libra. In this mansion make images of separation, destruction, desolation, allegation, and impediment.

Alichul, the seventeenth mansion at the end of Libra and the head of Scorpio, is the evil face of Venus. It is interpreted *Corona*. It starts at the end of the sixteenth mansion and concludes at eight degrees Scorpio. When Luna descends in this mansion, make images of discord, tribulation, and impediment.

Alcox, the eighteenth mansion in the heart of Scorpio, is the fortunate white face of Mercury. It starts at the end of the seventeenth mansion and concludes at twenty-one degrees Scorpio. When Luna descends in this mansion, make images of silence and the binding of tongues.

Alhebus, the nineteenth mansion at the tail of Scorpio and the head of Sagittarius, [86] which is to say the *acus*[3] or needle, is the fortunate white face

---

[1] *Sepher ha-Levanah* adds that the fourteenth mansion is the fortunate red and white face of Mercury.

[2] *Sepher ha-Levanah* has this mansion as the fortunate white face of Mars.

[3] "*Acus* or needle" *i.e.*, the stinger of the Scorpion, *al shaula*, the Arabic name of the nineteenth mansion.

of Luna.[1] It starts at the end of the eighteenth mansion and concludes at the fourth degree of Sagittarius. When Luna descends in this mansion, make images of fornication, sedition, allegation and lust.

Anahim, the twentieth mansion, the womb of Sagittarius, is the fortunate white face of Saturn. It starts at the end of the nineteenth mansion and concludes at seventeen degrees Sagittarius. When Luna descends in this mansion, make images to inspire love and concord.

Alberda, the twenty-first mansion at the end of Sagittarius, is the fortunate face of Jupiter. It starts at the end of the twentieth mansion and concludes at the last degree of Sagittarius. When Luna descends in this mansion, make images of cooperation. Also, in this mansion make images of silence.

Ceadaebyh, the twenty-second mansion at the head of Capricorn, is the evil unfortunate face of Mars, interpreted according to Aristotle as *desolation*. It starts at the beginning of Capricorn and concludes at twelve degrees Capricorn. When Luna descends in this mansion, make the images of a fortunate hour in which the face of Luna accords love, concord, and reflection. Or make images from the mansions where Luna is in discord to cause the division or departure of all good things.

Azatalbuta, the twenty-third mansion in the heart of Capricorn, is the face of *the fortune of the swallower*[2]; it is interpreted as the *fortune of fortunes*. It starts at the end of the twenty-second mansion and concludes at twenty-five degrees Sagittarius. When Luna descends in this mansion, make images of all good things.

Zadac Zahond, the twenty-fourth mansion at the tail of Capricorn and the head of Aquarius, is the *fortune of fortunes*[3], the most fortunate face of Venus. It starts at the end of the twenty-third mansion and concludes at eight degrees Aquarius. In this mansion, make an image of good, and it will be done.

Cealaghbrah, the twenty-fifth mansion in of the womb of Aquarius, is the fortunate white face of Mercury, the *fortune of tents*.[4] It starts at the end of the

---

[1] *Sepher ha-Levanah* has the nineteenth mansion as the unfortunate face of the Moon.

[2] The Arabic name for the twenty-third mansion is *al sa'd al bula*, which means "the good fortune of the swallower," so named because, according to Persian astronomer Al Kazwini (13th century), two stars near this constellation appear to *swallow* the light of each other.

[3] *Fortune of fortunes* – in Arabic, *al sa'd al su'ud*, "fortune of the fortunate," the Arabic name of the twenty-fourth mansion.

[4] *Tents* – in reference to the star Sadalachbia within the constellation Aquarius. The name is derived from the Arabic *al sa'd al ahbiyah*, "the luck of hidden things" or "the fortune of

twenty-fourth mansion and concludes at twenty-one degrees Aquarius. In this mansion, make images of silence and binding. Under this mansion you may bind whatever you wish.

Alfgarem, the twenty-sixth mansion at the end of Aquarius and the head of Pisces, is the fortunate face of Luna. It starts at the end of the twenty-fifth mansion and concludes at four degrees Pisces. When Luna descends [86v] in this mansion, make images of alliance, cooperation, friendship, or love of all things.

Alfgagir, the twenty-seventh mansion in the womb of Pisces, is an evil mansion and red face of Saturn. It starts at the end of the twenty-sixth mansion and concludes at seventeen degrees Pisces. When Luna descends in this mansion, make images of separation or departing, of binding, and of all infirmity.

Albecten, the twenty-eighth mansion at the tail of Pisces, the fortunate white face of Jupiter. It starts at the end of the twenty-seventh mansion and concludes at the last degree of Pisces. When Luna descends in this mansion, make images of all good things and of all profit, and any matter that you declare will go directly before the governors and be completed by commandment of the Creator.

---

tents." Al Kazwini called the central star of the Aquarian urn *Al Sa'd* and the three stars around it his "tents."

THE HOURS OF THE DAY AND NIGHT:

a paraphrase in contemporary English of *Liber Lunæ fols.* 87-92v

HOURS OF THE DAY

[87] Bolemus said that, when necessary, there is an operation for binding the tongues and hearts of accusers and envious men. On a talisman, make the image of the person whom you wish to constrain. On his forehead write the name of the mansion of the Moon of that time.[1] On the ridge [rim] of the talisman, write the name of the angel of the sign under which the operation is being done,[2] no matter whether this is done in a sign of the East, West, North or South; write these angel names and the names of their corresponding signs carefully, for the name by which God formed heaven, earth, sea, and all else is in them.[3]

Write the names to effect whatever you wish by the operation of binding — and of prosperity as well — of humans or beasts, wild fowls, and fish; engrave each part of it carefully. As for the angels, if you read the following names, your operation will surely work: *Lahagenim lagha laghoo layafurin uabalkanarithin laiagelm Laiaselesyn*. Saying these names aloud will compel a double effect. The angels which you call shall truly be bound to the sevice of any operation in which you use them, to give or take whatever you want.

"But," you may ask, "how should this be done?" When you intend to do the [87v] operation of the first hour, which concerns joining or binding, in the hour that you engrave the image on the talisman, read the names given above in their correct order. It is the same if you are performing an operation of expulsion: read the names in their correct order. Anyone who uses these names with the proper intent, at night, and hidden from others will not suffer distraction. Be very careful if you come into any unplanned difficulty

---

[1] Refer to § 1 of *Liber Lunæ*, MANSIONS OF THE MOON, or § (2) of *Sepher ha-Levanah*.

[2] The angels of the zodiac according to the table, SCALA DUODENARII, in Agrippa's *De occulta philosophia*, (LIBER SECUNDUS, CAP. XIV)—as shown in the edition prepared by Vittoria Perrone Compagni (Leiden: E. J. Brill, 1992), page 292, are as follows:

♈	Malchidael	♌	Verchiel	♐	Adnachiel
♉	Asmodel	♍	Hamaliel	♑	Hanaël
♊	Ambriel	♎	Zuriel	♒	Gabriel
♋	Muriel	♏	Barbiel	♓	Barchiel

[3] "The name by which God formed heaven, earth, sea, and all else is in them" – all of the angel names end with "el" [אל], meaning "God" or "of God."

with the operation in the hour that you engrave the names. Be sure to read the names in their correct order so that what you wish will truly occur, namely, that regions, cities, towns, and the houses of men and women be bound, or that birds, fish, or whatever you wish be constrained. If all is done correctly, you will profit by the power of the Creator. This is a true binding which must be hidden from all eyes, mouths, hearts, and tongues. The name of the first hour is *Vebiche*.

The operation of the second hour of any day is an operation of love, love requited, profit, and concord. Therefore, the image on the talisman of the second hour shows two heads on a conjoined body. The names of the lords of this hour are engraved on these heads. Carefully engrave the name of the hour on the breast of the image. The name of the lord of the hour should then be accurately written on the abdomen of the figure. The talisman should be made of fine wax showing the two-headed figure joined at the breast. After it is made, it should be buried next to your house; at the time of the burial, read the seven names given above in their correct order. Thereafter, whomever you intend will love each other evermore. These are the names: *Melkailin. Cadnaelin Amonayelin. farcelin. uorayeylin. affayelin. Badrayeylyn. Machiel. Canariel. Amymaryil. Fariel noreil azareil Batraiel*.[1] The name of the hour is *yenor*.

The third operation is done in the third hour of any day. It is said to be the operation of all fowls and fish. It is also for binding men or women— whomever you would bind. Write the seven precious names already given on the abdomen of the image, the name of the lord on the head, and the name of the hour on the breast. Suffume it with clean aloes and red sandalwood. Bury it in the vicinity of whom or what you wish to bind. Wonderful things will quickly come to pass in obedience to the commandment of God. Read the names of the first hour in the correct order. The name of the third hour is *Ansur*.[2]

The fourth operation is done in the fourth hour of any day. It is the operation of the silver serpent, or of scorpions, reptiles, and dragons. It is truly the operation of diverse wild beasts. On a talisman, make the likeness of the beast you wish to repel. Write the name of the lord of the hour on the breast and the seven names of the first hour on the abdomen. Bury it in the area where the beast resides, and it will leave that place. While you are engraving the seven

---

[1] These are presumably the names of the lords.

[2] No name is given for the third hour in the Sloane *Liber Lunæ*, just the word *answer* in parentheses (as shown in the transcription). Sloane MS 3826 *fol.* 78 gives *Ansur*. See Supplements to *Liber Lunæ* § 3. THE HOURS OF THE DAY AND NIGHT, below.

names of the first hour, read them aloud. The name of the hour is *Oelghil*.

The fifth operation is done in the fifth hour of any day. It is the operation of wolves, foxes, cats, and the like. The talisman should be made of silver on which is engraved the likeness of the beast you wish to control, with the name of it on its head and the name of the hour on its breast. Read the seven names of the first hour, and suffume the talisman with aloes. The name of the hour is *Coaleth*.

The sixth operation is done in the sixth hour of any day. It is an operation for captives and prisoners—anyone constrained. Perform this operation in the sixth hour using the image of a man with the name of the lord of the hour on the head, the name of the hour on the breast, and the seven names of the first hour on the abdomen. Always be careful to read the names of the first hour as Hermes has taught[1] during the suffumigation with aloes and red sandalwood. Make the image in the likeness of whomever you wish to deliver from captivity, one talisman for each captive. The name of the hour is *Juhunoe conchor*.

The seventh operation is done in the seventh hour of any day to gain strength and to obtain the opportunity to enter before kings, and from this meeting to receive admiration and love. The talisman should be made of silver showing an accurate likeness of the king whose audience is sought. Write the name of the king on the breast and the name of the lord of the hour and the seven names of the first hour on the abdomen. After it is made, carry the talisman upon entering before the king. The name of the hour is *Jador*.

The eighth operation is done in the eighth hour of any day. It is an operation against confusion and desperation so that whomever you wish may find shelter and reprieve. The image of the operation is that of a hound with two heads on a red brass talisman, one head being that of a man, the other that of a hound. Write the name of the man on the head, the name of the hour on the breast, and the seven names of the first hour on the abdomen. Suffume this with the blood or fat of a slain hound, then bury it where you like. You will see wonderful things. The name of the hour is *Jasolun* or *Jasumech*.

The ninth operation is done in the ninth hour of any day. It is for binding thieves. The talisman for this operation is made of silver showing the image of a man. Write the name of the thief on the head, the name of the hour on the breast, and the seven names mentioned above along with the names of the angels of obstruction on the abdomen. Suffume this with aloes and crocus

---

[1] "As Hermes has taught" = *in the correct order.*

and bury it where you would like to stop thieves. The thieves will change their minds, steal nothing, and depart. The name of the hour is *Baton* or *luron*.

The tenth operation is done in the tenth hour of any day. It is to loosen the tongues of kings, rich men—many kinds of men. Make a talisman of silver showing the figure of a man with the names of the angels of love and partnership, the name of the hour, and the name of the *second* hour. Suffume it with aloes and saffron fibers, as instructed above. Carry the talisman with you in a silk cloth and recite the seven names. The name of the hour is *Sachon* or *Sahon*.

The operation of the eleventh hour concerns restoring love between those who have had difficult relations. Make two talismans of silver at the appointed time, showing the names of the lords on their heads and the names of love—that is, the names of the second hour—on their breasts. Suffume this with pleasant aromas, aloes and saffron, burned slowly on a fire, and the two people who are the object of the operation will come to you and be reconciled. The name of the hour is *Jebrim*.

The twelfth operation is done in the twelfth hour of any day. It is to bind tongues. The talisman shows the likeness of the person whom you want to silence with the name of the lord on the head, the name of the hour on the breast, and the seven names on the abdomen. Suffumigation is done, as above, with aloes wood and saffron. Bury it in your own house wrapped in a clean white silk cloth on which is written *one i. normet*. Take the talisman of the second operation and, in the manner of a philosopher, hide yourself with it under the stars for seven nights, reading each night the seven names of the first hour, and suffume it each of these seven nights saying, "*Tu exumleazart et sandalos.*" The name of the hour is *Rabalon* or *vahialon*.

[90] Bolemus said that when Solomon questioned him, he was told to ordain for them a bath or a private fire.

The first hour of any night begins with an operation of baths or fires, or of silence. Take iron fused to brass. Make a wax vessel with four to six mouths[1]; on each mouth engrave these names: *Secesyn hayfaysyn harshin saluj seshin hershdiel remeahalyn Clodel Isus mahede*. On the underside of the vessel and in each of its mouths place a slip of paper which has been soaked in oil. On the underside of the vessel, which will not be seen, engrave these names: *Noryn badichin. Anadyn. Sibir sanaphinin. halkars. ahadichin anadyn. bahadin. Sanachin ranchbaili Jahudnil*. On the vessel put the image of a man holding a brass pot pouring out oil, and pour oil in the vessel itself using your left hand. Engrave on the image of the man these two names: *chichud* and *ephil*, the first on the abdomen and the second at the base of the vessel. Write *ib* אפ on all of the oiled papers, then burn them. Place a suitable cover over the vessel so that it will not be harmed. Or make the vessel with a hollow bottom, for then water put within it will remain hot forever. The name of the first hour of the night is *Cefratetyn* or *Hamon*.

The operation of the second hour of any night is done to banish fornication. [90v] Bolemus said that one must be within the city (referred to as *Laudarah*) in order to effectively perform this operation so that within it the women will never again fornicate. Start the operation by making a human figure on a talisman of clean brass and write on it these names: *Myant. chelem. faroc. kahumcul nohegemah*. On the face of the figure write *fecherah harsoleth iasad nadnad lecchat badah*. Note that the first group of names (beginning with *Myant*) should not be written over the whole image but upon a brass plate shown in the hand of the figure. Bury the talisman wherever a woman might fornicate, and, wherever it is buried, women will not fornicate. This operation can also affect the movement of water leeches, frogs, fish, and reptiles. The name of the hour is *Debzul* or *Canbuel*.

The third operation of the third hour of any night is done to control and contain beasts, such as serpents, scorpions, poisonous birds, hounds, mice,

---

[1] *Sepher ha-Levanah* indicates that this "vessel with four to six mouths" for the first hour of the night is a candelabrum or *menorah* with "seven mouths," and, instead of a slip of oiled paper, *Sepher ha-Levanah* has "wick."

It is difficult to visualize what is described here in Sloane MS 3826. What is intended might resemble the multiple-flame lamps of the early Roman period. See *Jewish Art Masterpieces from the Israel Museum*, edited by Iris Fishof (Jerusalem: The Israel Museum, 1994), pages 28-29.

etc. Make the image of the beast that you wish to control, and write upon its face these names: *Myatyon boroyon fafraril*. Bury it when and where you do not wish the beast to abide. The name of the hour is *Thaor*.

The fourth operation is done in the fourth hour of any night to destroy houses, towns, cities, and other structures [91] — wherever your enemies may dwell. Anoint the back of the talisman with camel urine kept within an urn, and write upon the talisman these words: *afflaceros ffeygiltans ffeyglah ceidarophin*. Then, say, "I adjure you that as this fire burns so will burn N (*the place you name*), the dwelling of N (*the person's name*) the son of N (*his mother's name*)" — you can name whoever or whatever place you will — then read the seven names, but letter by letter, for in doing so their secret will be maintained. The name of the hour is *Hallahay*.

The fifth operation is done in the fifth hour of any night to call forth destructive storms and to cause discord between men. The form used follows the above-mentioned two operations with the image of a double man, one of lead and the other of brass.[1] Engrave upon them these names: *Nesahælmiel Jeszarailin. Jszunielaie. atfamin renormen sekarkabel aragi mihan Jehabey bedyemyekalkel*. These are the names which will provoke whomever you wish. I can say to you truly that using these names brings great effect. There are also these names: *badakatir chen⁹syelchech*. Suffume the talisman and bury it in a high place. If you wish the destruction of a region or the imprisonment of someone, read the seven names in turn. The name of the hour is *Camfar*.

The operation of the sixth hour of whatever night is done to put any man out of his house. Make the talisman of red brass showing the image of the man you wish to expel. [91v] Write the names of expulsion on it. Suffume it and write the man's name on the head of the image. Then, put it in the house of the person for whom it was made, and he will flee to another region ten miles away being greatly perturbed and losing his wits. These are the names of expulsion: *belychiechyn Raysel. abrail. aflin. cadeneul. miamem. bafreni geraodin. barcaiol. analin. forachi. cafalin seche*. Other names with which to burn are *Amagnis*, etc. Write upon silk the seven names of the first hour and read them. The name of the sixth hour is *Zoran*.

The seventh operation is done in the seventh hour of any night for the combustion of grapes and the sap of trees. Make a talisman of red brass and engrave on it these names: ⅀⅂ ⅄ ; *pope per combustiones* ५4 ⋔H. *pir*

---

[1] The *Liber Lunæ* text has "2 operacions of a double man of 4te [quarter of a pound=115g] of lead s.r. pound and of brasse 2to [half a pound]." *Sepher ha-Levanah* also prescribes two separate images, one of lead and the other of brass, these being of equal weight: 65 drams.

ꝗ. 55 byablib. gehil combure d9 nissu et. Read the seven names in turn. Then, you should bury it at the time and place you wish to be burnt. Ten miles or more will be, by God's bidding, consumed by heavenly fire. The name of the hour is *Jafor*.

The eighth operation is done in the eighth hour of any night to gather male and female fowls in any manner you wish. Make the image of the fowl you desire on a talisman made of one ounce of the finest gold. Engrave on it these names: *Jerodah Carmetah adesach . achil . gabriel afferent vos ad me*, the final words of which [92] mean "Bring yourself to me." Bury the talisman in the highest place of the town in the right hour of the night. If you wish to gather other things, read the seven names and write this prayer: *ápes in oi loco et arte adducat vos Gabriel de diversis plagis*. Do the same for each thing you wish to gather. The name of the hour is *Myach*.

The ninth operation is done in the ninth hour of any night to gather fowls to a hill of your choosing. Make a talisman of one ounce of gold showing the likeness of what fowl you wish to gather. Write the names of the angels from the eighth operation on the abdomen. Once so engraved, bury the talisman, as in the eighth operation. Read the seven names in their proper order. The name of the hour is *Oritefor*.

The tenth operation is done, as above in the sixth hour, in the tenth hour to cause the departure of the haughty, those who love themselves, so that they are not a continuing annoyance. Make the talisman of this operation the length of your palm, and the four parts of it should be made of red brass. Actually, there are two medalions, one depicting the head of a female bear, the other depicting the head of a hound. Engrave their names upon their heads, and write the seven names of the first operation on the ridge [rim]. Suffume these with malodorous things. These are buried in different places, one on the east side and the other on the west side. Thus, all whom you wish to depart will do so. These are the names: *Gzorabi Izora hauli haule memoy nahualiemin matmoial* [92v] *kaihal malegen. moiogil. muctril muchil*. The name of the hour is *Malho*.

The eleventh operation is done in the eleventh hour of any night when you wish to draw a person to you or to repel him from you. Make the talisman as finely as possible of silver with the person's image on it. Engrave his proper name on the head and these names on the abdomen: *aragi rahian bedien Jahekalkel agnis kannaizozo maron kamerache emtelh amokoydar rasdar monras kaydich hartah*. Along with these names, carefully write this prayer: *Ignis de cælo combur per comburente ☉ com bureus bihu el alhalil combur jussu dei*. The name of the hour is *Aalacho*.

The twelfth operation is done in the twelfth hour of any night to cause torment and quaking in the body of whomever you wish. On a talisman of red brass make the image of a man with a large neck with his face in profile; put hands where feet should be and feet where hands should be. Write the name of the Lord on the head, the name of the planet on the breast, and engrave the following names on the ridge [rim]: *aeol alkeguh hun aguh maeraszach sagellesz mausz mahuh tortolaac Iblin*. Bury it at the gates of the person's house. The name of the hour is *fellen*.

a paraphrase in contemporary English of *Liber Lunæ fols.* 93-96v
with amended MAGIC SQUARES & other corrections

[93] Now follow the figures of the Planets

The figure of Saturn is a three-by-three square. Operations of this figure are done when the moon is increasing. In the first hour of Saturday, draw the figure on new cotton. Bind it to the thigh of a pregnant woman and she will face no danger and safely deliver her baby. If you suffume a piece of silk bearing this figure [93v] with frankincense and carry it with you, you need not fear either king or any other person who might attempt to impede you; you will get from them what you with. If you engrave this figure on lead, whether Saturn is retrograde, direct, or stationary, and put it in a new building or plantation, this place will never be filled with people; indeed, men will flee from it. If you put it on the seat of a prelate, he will be deposed from this office—but only if the magical inscription is first written above or next to the figure.

The figure of Jupiter is a four-by-four square in which the sum of any rank or column is 34. On a Thursday in the hour of Jupiter, when Jupiter is direct, make this figure on a silver disk. Suffume it with aloes wood and amber. Carry it with you, and everyone whom you see will love and obey you. If you put the disk between the feet of a merchant, his business will increase. And if you put it in a pigeon house or bee hive, the pigeons or bees will gather. If one who is unfortunate carries it with him, he will become fortunate, improving quickly. If you put it on the seat of a prelate, he will reign long and prosper against all of his enemies, and they will not trouble or frighten him. [94] Do not forget to put the magical inscription above the figure.

The figure of Mars is a five-by-five square in which the sum of every rank and column is 65. It signifies war and destruction. On a Tuesday in the hour of Mars, when Mars is retrograde, combust, or diminished, engrave its figure on a copper disk. Suffume it with menstrual blood, with the clothing of one who has been hanged, with the sword of one who has been slain, or with mouse or cat dirt. Put it in a new house or building and it will not be fruitful; rather, it will be barren. If it is put on the seat of a prelate, he will decline quickly. If the disk is put in the place of a merchant, it will destroy his business completely. If you make this figure in the name of two men who love each other and bury it in the house of either of them, hate and enmity will fall between them. If you engrave the copper disk while Mars is direct or increasing, suffume it with red silk and saffron, and wrap it in the same red silk and pack it with frankincense—even better cornelius—then, in its presence, neither great lords nor enemies can harass you; they will be doomed in battle and will flee at the sight of you. They [94v] will dread you and be ashamed. If you put a virgin parchment bearing this figure on the thigh of a woman, she will menstruate. If you put it where bees are, they will fly away. Engrave the magical inscription above the figure.

1	32	34	3	35	6
30	8	27	28	11	7
10	24	15	16	13	23
19	17	21	22	18	24
10	26	12	9	29	25
31	4	2	33	5	26

figura Solis

The figure of the Sun is a six-by-six square in which the sum of every rank and column is one-hundred eleven. It concerns the kings and princes of this world—all lordship and power. When the Sun is in its exaltation in the fifth degree of Aries, take six drams of pure gold and make a round disk. On a Sunday in the hour of the Sun, engrave the figure of the Sun on the gold disk. Suffume it in musk and camphor, and wash it in rosewater, musk, and camphor. Wrap it in yellow silk and carry it with you and it will cause whatever you wish to happen: You will get from rich men whatever you want. You will be honored among kings and great lords, and whatever you ask for will be given. Whatever you clearly visualize will be granted to you.

4	35	10	41	16	47	22
29	11	41	17	48	23	8
12	36	18	49	24	6	30
37	18	43	25	7	31	13
20	44	26	1	32	14	38
45	27	2	33	8	39	21
28	3	34	9	40	15	46

figura veneris

The figure of Venus is a seven-by-seven square in which the sum of each rank and column is 175. It concerns [95] one's fortunes with women and love. When Venus, direct or stationary, is in Pisces, which is its exaltation, or in Taurus or Libra, which are its houses, it is fortunate and swift in effect. On a Friday in hour of Venus, take seven drams of pure silver and make a disk; suffume it with aloes wood, amber, and mastic, and put it in a white silk cloth, and you will see marvels. If a man or woman lingers unmarried, let him or her carry the disk, and he or she will soon be wed. If someone hates you, wash the disk bearing this figure with rainwater, well water, or rosewater, and give the water to the one who hates you to drink, and he will love you. If you are agitated, wash the figure with chamomile water and sprinkle this water in the place where there is dread or discord, and all evil will cease and there will be peace and wisdom. If you sprinkle this water where animals or merchandise are, they will multiply and increase. If you put it in your bed, you will come to be *in coitu* and you will be loved.

figura Mercurij

8	7	59	60	61	62	2	1
49	15	54	12	53	51	10	16
41	42	22	21	20	19	47	48
32	34	35	29	28	27	39	36
40	26	27	37	36	30	31	33
17	18	46	45	44	43	23	24
9	55	14	52	13	22	50	45
64	63	3	4	5	6	58	57

The figure of Mercury is an eight-by-eight square in which the sum of each rank and column is 260. Mercury is very swift and enchanting; it has the nature [95v] of all of the other planets and the qualities of all of the signs. Mercury bears the strength of the soul and the wisdom of life. On a Wednesday in the hour of Mercury when Mercury is direct in its course, make a disk with eight drams of pure silver, and engrave on it the figure of Mercury. Suffume it with aloes wood, cloves, and mastic; carry it with you and anything that you ask for you will have. If you do not have silver, make it of citrine paper, which works as well. If you put it in a place of prelacy or on the chair of a prelate, he will endure against his enemies, and his allies will increase. If you put the figure on a ring of glass, in a basin, or on a glass disk in the first hour of Wednesday in the first seven days of lunation, cast it into a well, and then drink from this well three days in a row, all forgetfulness will leave you, and you will learn anything you wish easily. If you put the figure on a steel mirror, anyone who has the palsy or seizures will be cured just by looking at it. Anyone who is blinded from venereal disease will similarly be cured. Another method is to fast by three days in a row, eating only bread and honey; after that, draw the figure of Mercury on citrine silk, suffume it with aloes wood, and say: "O God, by the virtue of this figure, show me in my dreams what I wish to know." [96] Then, put it under your pillow when you lie down. But first, write the magical inscription above the figure.

37	78	29	70	21	62	13	54	5
6	38	79	30	71	22	63	14	46
47	7	39	80	31	72	23	55	15
16	48	8	40	81	32	64	24	56
57	17	49	9	41	73	33	65	25
26	58	18	50	1	42	74	34	66
67	27	59	10	51	2	43	75	35
36	68	19	60	11	52	3	44	76
77	28	69	20	61	12	53	4	45

figura Lunæ

The figure of the Moon is a nine-by-nine square in which the sum of each rank and column is 369. On Monday in the hour of the increasing Moon, draw on virgin parchment the figure of the Moon with ink of musk and saffron tempered with rosewater. Suffume it with cucumber extract and camphor. Fold the parchment in half and put it in a silver tube and carry it with you. This figure also promotes the fulfillment of all noble things and takes away evil. If you dread an enemy, put this figure in his path, and you will be delivered from the enemy and all evil. To this end, draw the figure on a large parchment of sheepskin with the blood of a black cock that is gelded on a Monday when the Moon is in its diminution; on the side, carefully draw the figures of Pisces and Cancer with same blood mentioned; put the parchment in a little pot full of water, and let it stand overnight in the air. On the following day, take the pot and say, "Go out N (*the name of your enemy*), the son of N (*the name of his mother*), from N (*his place or city*), may he never return." Repeat this holding the water to all four parts of the world, namely, once each to the East, South, West, and North.

To prevent a woman from being [96v] wed, on a disk of lead draw the figure during the Moon's diminution on a Monday in the hour of the Moon, saying, "I bind N (*the name of the woman*), the daughter of N (*the name of her mother*), that she never wed nor bear children." On the other side of the disk, make the image of the woman. Then, bury it in the sepulcher of an unknown man. If you can not sell your merchandise, draw the figure with saffron tempered with rosewater on citrine paper during the Moon's increasing on a Monday in the hour of the Moon. Suffume it with cucumber extract and camphor and fold the paper in half. Put it with the things to be sold or on the neck of an animal, and they will be sold soon at a good price, thanks to God. These are the names mentioned: *niselesayal nilegayal Nihtiranaklaban nirufayal oohgal ahgal ninegiohal.*

NOTE ON THE TRANSCRIPTION OF THE NEXT TWO SECTIONS:

Spellings (like *kemyng* for *combing*), abbreviations (*e.g.*, ☉ to mean the image or talisman of the work), superscript additions ("^being^horoscopo") and words struck through (*e.g.*, ~~Bas~~), are kept as in the original.

Superscript is also used for scribal conventions (*e.g.*, wch for *which*, p^arty for *party*. Variations on the shorthand

[80] *Cu volueris ligare latrines vt non &c*
When thou wylt bynde theeves that they enter not into any house when the
first face were of *Alhamel* that is to say Ariets ascendant and Luna make the
ymage of a man of brasse And when thymage were p^arfite or fulfilled then
say thou *Alligo œm latrine ab hac domo per hanc* ☉ And bury it in the middle of
the house and he shall not enter w^thout end.

That kyne dwell still upon calves under the same horoscope That is under
the first face of ♈ and Luna in the same ascendant make ☉ of a calf of brasse
saying *Ligo œm vacca p hanc* ☉ *vt qu enq super ea transierit non recedat.* Be it
burned where thou wylt.

That fyer tende or kindle not under the same horoscope make ☉ of a man
Coprin or of Copper the head of wch be upon the head of an Hounde wth w^ch
be a candlesticke saying *Ligovi igno ab hac domo vt non accentdat^or in ea in
æterna* that it be not tende or kindle in it w^thout end Be it buried at thy liking.

[80v] That a woman sit kemyng her head under the same horoscope make ☉
of copper holding in her hand a Combe saying *Non transeat sup^er istam
imagine mulier quin sedeat pecteus caput sum* That is to say Ne passe thou not
upon this Image a woman that ne she sit kemyng her head Be it buryed at
thy liking in the way in wch they passe ffor there shall not passe a woman
that ne shall discover her head frotting it that her haires fall

ffor to bynde serpents Under the same horoscope being the second face of
Alkebs that is to say Ariets ascending make ☉ of a serpent brazen or of brasse
saying I have bound eche serpent that in this place they let no man or this
Ligavi œm serpente^svt in isto loco neiem impediant. Be it buried in the middle
place divided.

That the members of a man be bound under the same horoscope being the
third face of *Alhamel* ascending of brasse ☉ of a man upright saying *Ligavi te
Socrate^s seu fronicu^s vt cu aliqua coire non possis* That is to say I have bound thee

Socrates or fronicus that wth any thou go not togither or might not go togither, be it buried in a dry pitt.

That a man have fever Under the same horoscope being the third face of *Alhamel* ascending that to whome thou wilt fevers take, be there graven ⊙ an ymage of a man in a plate of tynne wth this orison. *sicut es figura* ⊙ *Socratis seu fronici sic accipiant eu febres vel demones* that is to say As thou art the figure of worching [81] of Socrates or fronicus so take him fevers or divels In the sea of water it is to be buried.

That an enemy enter not in a City. Under the first face to Taurus horoscope being make ⊙ of a man having a sword in the hand in the first face of the hower being saying *Ligavi hanc Civitate vt non expuguet eam inimicus in æternu neg exercitus*. That is to say I have bound this City that an ememy fight not against it w^thout end neither an hoast. And then be it buried in the 4 p^arts of the City in the middle of the same.

That locke open. Under the second face of Taurus ^being^horoscopo ~~being~~ that Solution be made of locke Iron saying *Solvo seras tactas cu* ⊙ *ista*. That is to say I loose locke touched wth this worching. And standing the locke shall be opened.

That hounds barke not Under the 3 face of ♉ the hower being make ⊙ of an hounde of lead, and have he it wth him, and go he surely among hounds.

That an horse stand. Under the third face of ♉ make ⊙ of an horse of lead Saying *non transeat super istam figura equus quin stet*. That is to say Ne passé there not upon this figure an horse that ne he stand, and be it buried at thy liking in the third face of ♉

That a minstrell be distrayned under the [81v] second face of ♊ the hower being make ⊙ of a man of waxe or of brasse some instrum^ent holding saying *Non canat Joculator vbi hæc* ⊙ *fuerit quin disfruant^e ejus instrumenta duc inter eos* That is to say Ne sing not a minstrell where this worching were that ne instruments of him be destroyed, led betwixts them.

Ut hortus non faciat fructu sub eode &c
That a gardeine make not fruit. Under the same make ⊙ of a tree upon wch be ⊙ of a serpent of Copper. About the serpent be there wormes saying *Ligavi hunc hortu vt fructu non faciat* That is to say I have bound this garden that it make not fruite. And be it buried in the garden and wormes shall eat all.

That whome thou lovest follow thee. Under the second face of Cancer the hower being make ⊙[1] of a woman of Tyme or waxe saying *Attraxi cor N fil: mris ad ineipsu propter amore et dilectionem et provocavi spni ejus provocatione forti vt meus ignis et ejus virtus et sicut provocatione venti et ejus ffatus.* Touche whome thou lovest and she shall follow thee obeying to thee If not hang it in an high tree, and thou shalt see marvells And blowe ⊙ when thou seeth these.

That a wall fall Under the third face of Cancer the hower being make a wall of lead saying [82] *Cadat ois paries apud quem sepeliatur ista* ⊙ *et cadet iste sub que sepeliat*[r] That is to say eche wall fall anentis the wch this ⊙ is buried. And this shall fall under wch this is buried.

That haile fall not. Under the 3 face of Cancer the hower ascending make ⊙ of a wenche all in lead, in the hand of whome be haile saying *Non transeat super* ⊙ *ista grando loco vbi fuerit sepulta et non cadet ibi grando* That is to say ne passe there not upon the ⊙ haile in the place where it were buried at thy liking.

That a man be made sicke. Under the second face of Leo the hower being *infirmitate accipiat N fil: N mris febris vel quævis infirmitas deinde in pelago* make ⊙ of a man of brasse or tynne raising his hands saying *Pro qualibel subhumetur.* That is to say ffor each infirmity take the son of N. of N. mother fevers of what sicknes thou wylt. And then be it buried in the sea, or be it put under the treen betill of a better and say to the heat that dolor and heate take the head of him.

That a field bring not fruite Under the first face of Virgo, the hower being make ⊙ of a woman of tynne or of lead or of earth, and put In his right hand 2 eares of Corne that he hold them saying *Ligavi hunc agru vt non naseatur in eo messis* That is to say I have bound this field that corne waxe not in it, be it buried in the field & it shall never beare fruit of the kynde that is in the hand of ye ymage.

[82v] That ravens be gathered togither. The first face of Virgo the hower being make ⊙ of half a raven, and another halve deale under the second face of Virgo saying *Non remaneat Corbus nisi veniat ad hanc* ⊙ That is to say Ne remayne there not a raven but he come to this ⊙ or ymage Be it buried to thy liking.

---

[1]   This sentence is underlined in the MS.
    In the left margin at this place:
        sub 2^a facie
        ♋^i *horoscopo*
        existente
        fac opus vel
        Imaginē

That a shepe stand. Under the third face of Virgo ascending the hower being make ⊙ of a man of tynne having wth him a litl bell saying upon yt. *Nonremaneat Ovis vel Capra transiens super eam quiu stet.* That is to say Ne remayne there not a sheepe or a goate passing upon yt that he ne stand Be he buried at thy liking.

That workemen worke not any thing Under the second face of Virgo make of a man of waxe wth so many instruments that thou wilt bynde saying to everich when thou wilt bynde In wch place were wont to be done And say that they werche not any thing.

That there be not sold any thing in the tent – In the first face of ♎ ascending make ⊙ of a man holding in the hand *libram* saying *Ligavi hoc tentoriu vt abijciat ab eo hoies vt non vendatur aliquio in eo durat ⊙ hic sepulta* That is to say. I have bound this tent that he cast from him men. That any thing be not sold in yt while ⊙ dureth buried heere.

[83] *Ligatio regis pro malo secunda facie Libræ &^c*
Bynding of a king for evill In the second face of Libra the hower being make ⊙ of a king of lead sitting upon a benche and in environ of him make keep^ers saying *Ligavi hunc rege N perista ⊙ ab hac regione vt non in ea malu faciat neg ererceat in ea injurias.* That is to say I have bound this king N by this ⊙ or working from this region that he do not evill in it neither use in it iniuryes. In the middle of a region or of a city be it buryed.

That thou take fishes In the second face of Libra the hower being make ⊙ of a ship of lead full of fishes saying *non remaneut pisces quiu veniat ad hanc ⊙* That is to say Ne remayme there not a fishe that ne he come to this ⊙ or working Be it buried in the river.

That a man make himself bare or naked. Under the second face of Scorpius the hower being make ⊙ of a man naked of brasse saying *Non transeat super hanc ⊙ aliquis quiu proijciat vestimenta sua et nudus remaneat* That is to say Ne passe there not upon this ⊙ any man that he ne cast away his Clothes and remayne bare or naked. Be it buried at thy liking.

That a man or a woman passe not that ne he sing and play, the first face of Capricorne make ⊙ of a wenche of tynne In the hand of her be a plate of tynne saying *non transeat super ista* [83v] *⊙ vir neg mulier quiu cantet et ludat* That is to say Ne passe there not upon this ⊙ a man nor a woman that he ne sing and play. Be it buried in the way at thy liking where women passeth.

That flyes fly from an house. Under the second face of Aquarius the howere being make ⊙ of a fly in the stone of a ring either of gold or silver and about

⊙ these words be written *Non vides musca quæ aderit quavis mille milliu essent locu illu derelinquent et mors configet eis. deinde eo dicente musca moriamini* That is to say thou shalt not see a fly that shall abide although there were a thousand thousand they shall forsake that place and death shall befall to them. And then he saying flyes be ye dead The ring be it discovered in the house and they should fly.

ffor to bynde a taverne or to agast write these names in virgin p^archement and bynde wth a thred of brasse to some post in the taverne. *uriel. hobiel. dodiel uriel daniel kauael salguel michael assiduel duriel conjuro vos angelos fortes vt removeatis œmhoiem q non posset accedere ad Taverna ista ad emendu aliquid in eo. Conjure vos per angelu forte qui a Deo diligitur super œs et est sine fine Amen.* That is to say I coniure yo^u strong angels that ne remayne eche man that he may not come nigh to this taverne to buy any thing in it. I coniure yo^u by the strong Angell wch is loved of God upon all. And he is w^thout end.

Work of the hours

a. Sloane MS 3826 *fols.* 65-67v

[65]

Cum volneris subsᶜcribbere ad odin~ aspice solem &ᶜ
When thou wilt write to hate behold thou the sonne and the day of him ffor
if thou fyndest it in ♈ ♌ or ♐ worke thou to hate in the first hower of the
same for it is the hower of solis. And write thou the name of the day and the
name of the hower and the Charact[er] of Solis wᶜʰ be thend of this booke
nempning the sepᵃʳation or depᵃʳting betwixt everich either pᵉʳson seethe this
scripture is full necessary And if it befalleth that ♂ be wᵗʰ ☉ it shall be
stronger to this that thou wilt worche And work thou not but if ☉ be in fiery
signes And worke thou nothing in other howers of the same day.

[65v] The day of Luna the first hower of same is to write in it Þ¹ to entering
upon kings and axe thy things and change thou what things thou wylte. And
be thou warefor the coming betweene of Luna to Caput draconis that is in
the first knott fro it is secret & hid Also when it cometh to the second knott
and the third And be thou ware from other knottes if sothely thou wilt worke
to payne & perdition worke thou by the fowre last knottes. And when Luna
were in any of these thy worke shall be fulfilled in thine axing.

And the viᵗʰ hower of the day of Luna in veneris. Therfore worke thou in it to
love and the viiᵗʰ of the same is of ♀ worke thou in it to dilection of men
togither. And the day of Luna accordeth generally to eache worke that thou
wilt And most if Luna were in ♉ or ♋ or ♓ And if ♀ were wᵗʰ it thy worke
shall be stronger and it shall helpe to suffer betwixt the man and the woman
Therfore worke thou all these on diminution of Luna

The day of ♂ the first hower of it when therefore thou wilt make sicke any
man or woman wᵗʰ divers torments in bynding or losing of body or taking
away of wytt or what ever thou wilt any man suffer in his body thy work
shall be fulfilled and thou shalt fulfill in it Therfore dread thou God and let

---

¹ The letter shown (Þ) here and below in the paragraph on the day of Jupiter is the Old
English letter *thorn*, "th." It is unclear what it represents here.

not a true man and worke thou in the first hower of the day of ♂ and write what thou wilt. After that thou hast written the name of the man & the name [66] of the day and the name of the hower and the name of ♂ and write thou the characts of ♂ and wth all this thou shalt fulfill

The second hower of it is of ☉ worke thou in it like to this when ☉ werein his fiery signes And write thou the names as I have beforesaid to the charact[er]s of ☉ and the name And if ♂ were in ♏ bynde thou serpents & scorpions. And the third hower is of ♀ worke thou in it to all love when he were in his fortune or exaltation for then it shall be sharper in this thing. Thou shalt write the name of the hower of it and of the day and the charact[er]s of it for thou shalt profitt. And the 4th hower is of ☿ write in it to hate and departing and thou shalt write the charact[er]s of ☿ and the names as it is said in other planets

The day of ☿ the first hower is of it of wch the empire is strong when it were in his exaltation worke thou in the hower of privy things. And the 2 hower is of ☽ write thou in it to peticions of ☿ And worke thou not in other howers of this day any thing.

The day of ♃ the first hower of it is write Þ in it to kings and enter thou upon them when ♃ were in[1] And bynde thou shippes that were in the sea And if ☽ were wth it, it shall be stronger in all things that thou shalt worke in kings and of other & to concord betweene them that be attwayne And worke thou in it to love of women when he were in his fortune. And write the names & characters after that I have before said to thee And the 2 hower is of ☿ write & affliction of him that thou wylt. And the 3 is of ☽ worke thou in it to divers & all things that thou wilt.

[66v] The day of ♄ the first hower of it is worke thou in it to all odible works betweene friends, do all worke that thou wilt in the same hower of waxe and Lute. And if thou wilt make a man sicke take of the clothes of him if thou might & write in them the working of the man & the name of the hower, & the name of the day. and cast into a fyer that is not quenched as the fier of a bath & of and oven and this shall be the sicknes of him. And if then ♄ were in his fortune or in his exaltation the worke of him shall be stronger.

The first hower the name of it is *hebiem* the second *luuer*. The third *Camu*. The fourth *telgilim* the fifth *Tathalit*. The sixth *Tenhor*. The 7th *Jador*. The 8th *Jafatu*. The 9th *Baron* The 10th *Jahon*. The 11th *Jebron*. The 12th *aliachalon*.

[1] There is a space in the manuscript here.

In the first hower is made orison of men to their God It is good in it to bynde all tongs

In the second is made the orisons of angells to the Lord and in the same be made works of concord or dilection or love betweene men and to all creatures of eache spirit.

In the third fowles bringeth thankings to their Lord In it be made the works of fowles and of fishes

In the 4th creatures do thankings to their Lord In it be made the works of serpents & of scorpions.

In the 5th eache beast doth thankings to the Lord In it be made the workes of wolves & of wilde beasts fowre footed

In the 6th is made the orison of Cherubin to their Lord for [67] encreasing of all things and of incantations And in it be made the works of them that is prisoned and they be delivered.

In the 7th is made the orison of them that fasteneth the throne.

In the 8 be made the workings of departings & strife beside creatures.

In the 9th be made the workings of traveling men that theeves lett them not neither go out to them wthout end.

In the 10th waters singeth to their lord and in yt descendeth the spirit of the Lord and he maketh to tremble, and the worke of taking of kings be made and entring to them, and they should not speake to him evill. And if water were taken in yt and were medled to an oyntment made holy or hallowed and wth this he were annoynted that suffereth spasmu it shall profitt to him bythe comanndem[en]t of God almighty.

In the xith just men be glad. And in it be made the works of love and of concord.

In the xiith men be outcast and in it be made the works of sylence that they speake not furthermore upon whome they be made.

Si quis maxima dilectionis reverentiæ et benignitatis &c
Who ever willeth himself to be seene and be had of most dilection reverence & benignity in the hower of ♃ in the day of him ☉ be it fused of brasse and that most privily and wth cleannesse and grave he his name in ☉ wch avoideth wth the ayre, and wth good odors be it filled. And this orison among there ne leave he not *O Jou fulgen tissimu sps neg in honore et dilectione populi et maxima poteste sublevate corda potelintu voluntates* [67v] *hoinm meæ voluntati*

convenire, And when that is done be it wrapped in cleane clothes and in the Cloth be paynted the seale of Jovis And in the middle of the city in wch he willeth to be, be it burned. If sothely thou wilt make concord make ☉ in the howre of Jou or of some lving Joue, and one clepe that other and be it put Under the earth togither. And the foresaid orison Be it not leaved or be it not still for any love added If sothely any man would be holden wth the love of any woman make he ☉ in the hower of ♃ and in his day and o[?][1] of him in the hower of ♀ or be it[2]　　　　or be it paynted in most cleane and white p^archement. And his name in the head of the planet and in the brest, and that one kisse that other and clepe. And about the head seales of the planets be they paynted, And when this is done be they suffumed wth thure & croco and in the hower of action this orison be it not leaved *O Jovis et Veneris amabileset grales sps amore .S. cordi illius adtubetesup* ☉ *meam cordi ejus imprimite ut quandiu res ista duraverit se mitri ad voluntate mraexhibeat potentiaq creatoris.* And then if it be metall in the responsory of this to wch it is direct be they putt under the earth if paynted upon him to whome the love neded & besides the beholding of him for whome it was made.

---

[1] The script is unclear here.
[2] There is a space in the manuscript here.

b. Sloane MS 3826 fols. 78-80

[78] *Dixit Bolemus ph*[ilos] *de hijs quæ p*[o] *neccia sunt &*[c]

Bolemus the ph[ilosoph]er said of these that first be necessary the names of dayes and of night of howers when it is necessary to pray by them and to seche helpe by the natures of them for strength of them by the Comanndement of God.

Knowe thou therefore that the first of howers of everiche day is nempned *Vehich*, in it men pray to their Creato[r] and it is able to bynding of all things

The second hower is named *yeror*. In it Angells pray their Creato[r], and in this hower be made the worchings of love and of concord betweene all maner Creatures and men and coniunction of spirits

The third is named *Ansur*. In it fowles do thankes to their Creato[r]. In this be made the worchings of fishes and of all fowles.

The fourth is named *Oelgil*. In it Creature do thanks to their Creato[r]. In it be made the worchings of serpents of scorpions and of Dragons.

The fifth is named *Coaleth* In it all beasts do thanks to their Creato[r]. In it be made the worchings of wolves of cattes and of all wylde beasts.

The sixth is named *Coulher* In it prayeth Cherubin for the synnes of men. In it be made the worchings of Becends*[1] and of men to be delivered.

The seventh is named *Jador* In it prayeth Seraphin [78v] bearing the throne. In it be made the workings of concord betwixt kings.

The eight is named *Jasumah*. In it be made worchings betwixt men.

The ix[th] is named *Luron*. In it is made worchings of them that goeth a pilgrimage least theeves let them neither go out to them w[th]out end.

The x[th] is named *Sahon*. In it water singeth to his Lord. In it descendeth the spirit of God, and it maketh ighen to quake. In it be made worchings taking kings when any man entreth to them that they speake not evill to him. And of water be taken the same hower and medled to an ointment hallowed, and eche that suffreth a wicked spirit were annoynted he shall be healed by the Comanndement of God.

---

[1] "Becends" seems to be a plural of "besend," which form (using the prefix *be-*) is usually a verb. Here it means the *causing of things to be sent*.

The eleventh is named *Relimj* In it Just men be glad. In it be made the worchings of love and of Concord and of dilection

The xii[th] is named *Vahialon*. In it is made m[er]ciablenes of men. In it be made workings of silence that he speake not w[th]out end upon whome this worke were.

> *The names of the howers of y[e] night in w[ch] worchings*
> *made be more worth and more mighty then the*
> *working of the day by much.*

The first hower is nempned *Hamon* w[ch] I found in another *diacholym*. In it is made the orison of divels to their Creato[r] and they lett no man till they be raised from the Orison and in this hower be made the worchings of sylence.

[79] The second is named *Canbeul*. In this hower be made the worching of fishes and of water leches and of Crocdiles and of froggs and of all water beasts that they be not moved

The third is named *Thabor* in it singeth beasts in it be made worchings that fire burne not and of dragons and serpents that they lett not And in it is bounden eache long that it speake not.

The fourth is named *Alahan*. In it were divells upon sepulchers, of this is made dread and if a man offendeth or graveth them he shall dread and the haires of him shalbe raised and quaking he shall dread from them. And in this hower be made worchings that be graven in gold and silver and concord and love in croco and rubeo that is in saffron & red and of all Impediment and evill.

The fifth is named *Camifer* In it goeth water and Creatures singeth. In it be made workings of evill clouds and of huge wyndes.

The sixth is nempned *Zaron*. In it resteth the water and is ceased, and if there were ravished of it in the same hower and medled to the oyntmt of priests hallowed, and they that have fevers were annoynted wth it w[ch] sleepeth not sound sleepe and rest by the Comandmt of God. In it be made the worchings of Dreames by w[ch] it shall be seene in dreames what is to be done in good and evill.

The 7[th] is nempned *Cafor* in it be made the [79v] worchings of kings that who ever axeth any thing of them and they letteth him not, and they should not deny any thing w[th]out end by the Comandement of God.

The viii[th] is named *Cinach*. In it seeds of the earth prayeth the highest God. In it be made the worchings of meads and of gardens and of trees, and of all maner seeds of the earth that they be abled and kept from all Impediments by the sufferance of God.

The ix^th is named *Oroostafar*. In it be made workings of Angels to the Lord of worlds. and in it be made the workings of ingoings to kings and of buildings, the tongues of men and the other Creatures and of away putting the Impediment of them.

Th x^th is named *Malho*. And it is profitable in it to be made workings that a woman do not fornication or women of all a region

The xi^th is named *Alaacho*. In it be opened the gates of heaven wth orisons who ever enclepeth his Lord God shall give that he axeth. In it be made the worchings of most concord and of love durable to weddings &^c And it in it be smitten togither the wings of fowles and of Cocks whereof it is named *Aalaco* And it is of all the over p^arty of the earth And in it waxeth the sonne upon the Creature of God of the high Paradice.

The xii^th is named *fellen* In this hower resteth the hoast of heavens light gives while men praseth their highst Creato^r. And in it be made the workings of silence and of religion. And it is cleped the worke [80] of stonyng and of gastenes who that beholdeth it amased and astonyed as a man out of wytt he is troubled and he may not speake. And that that were done in this hower of worke shall not be losed of any man w^thout end, and this now is proved. There be made sothely 4 Sutyl. tynnyn. sylverii and ~~Bas~~ Brassyn And nothing may adnull of them any thing of the fyrst and the last.

APPENDIX

SLOANE MS 3826 57^R — 83^V

INTRODUCTION

This section of Sloane MS 3826 consists of

1. Names (*ff* 57-57v)
2. *Incipit Canon*: The rule of the book of consecration, or the manner of working (*ff* 58-60)
3. Orisons (*ff* 60-65)
4. Magical directions (*ff* 65-83v)

Arthur Waite refers to Sloane MS 3826[1], noting, "The independent treatises which follow the *Sepher Raziel* in Sloane MS 3826 extract matter from the *Sworn Book* [of Honorius]." Robert Mathiesen[2] lists "Sloane MS 3826...*ff* 58-83?" [Mathiesen's question mark] among the manuscript versions of the SWORN BOOK at the British Library, though he places it with those which "preserve the original Latin text." Portions of 3826 are in Latin, such as the orisons and some opening lines transcribed here, but the bulk of the text is in Early Modern English, circa 1564.

In the introduction to *Liber Iuratus Honorii*,[3] Gösta Hedegård refutes the identification with the *Sworn Book*, quoting Rachel Stockdale that 3826 *ff* 58-62 contains "[t]he rule of the booke of Consecration or the manner of working, with some orisons." Hedegård then refers to Waite (*Book of Black Magic...*, page 35, which is an earlier edition of *Book of Ceremonial Magic*), stating that the treatises of this part of 3826 "extract matter" from Honorius works; Hedegård allows that this "may possibly be right" (page 14, note 13).

---

[1] *Book of Ceremonial Magic, Including the Rites and Mysteries of Goetic Theurgy, Sorcery and Infernal Necromancy* London: William Rider & Son, Ltd, 1911, page 23

[2] "A Thirteenth-Century Ritual to Attain the Beatific Vision from the *Sworn Book* of Honorius of Thebes," *Conjuring Spirits: Texts and Traditions of Medieval Ritual Magic*, edited by Claire Fanger, University Park: Pennsylvania State University Press, 1998: p. 145.

[3] *Liber Iuratus Honorii: A Critical Edition of the Latin Version of the Sworn Book of Honorius*, ACTA UNIVERSITATIS STOCKHOLMIENSIS: *Studia Latina Stockholmiensa*, Stockholm: Almquist and Wiksell International, 2002, pages 13-14, note 37).

While there are similarities in content and form, I found no direct correlation between the Sloane MS 3826 passages and the version of *Liber iuratus* at Joseph Peterson's website, TWILIT GROTTO.[1]

NOTES ON THE TRANSCRIPTION

Spellings (one place *worching,* another *working*), abbreviations (*noie* for *nomine, sctissimis* for *sanctissimis,* etc.), and words struck through (*e.g.,* ~~Bas~~) are kept as in the original.

Superscript is used for certain conventions (*e.g.,* wch for *which,* p^arty for *party* where ⅋ means *par* or *per*).

The text begins mid-page at *folio* 57.

---

[1] www.esotericarchives.com/juratus/juratus.htm

[57]

And heerafter beginneth names that be necessary to everiche xpen man.
Hæc sunt 4 noia creatoris et unumquodg est &ᶜ

These be the 4 names of the creatoᵣ and everiche is of 4 letters, and prophets beare them written in precious stones. And these be the names Jobac Jona Eloy yena. And knowe thou that who ever beareth these names written in parchmyn that in Hebrew is named Gauil in golden lres with him lyflood and clothing worshipfully lacketh not him, how long he hath them with him.

A name to get victory
Hoc est nomen cum quo Josue fecit &ᶜ

This is the name wᵗʰ wᶜʰ Josue made the sonne [57ᵛ] to stand in his place against his proper nature wᵗʰ wᶜʰ he overcame gabionitas 34 kings. And this is a great name and virtuous dreadfull and gastlewe Bachianodobalizlior and this Bachianodobalizlior hac. And this name giveth vengeannce of enemyes. And who that ever beaeth it wᵗʰ him a prison may not hold him neither in battaile he may be overcome wᵗʰ any man.

To gladnes and against wrath & Ire
Hoc est nomen q dixit Creator Moisi &ᶜ

This is a name that the Creator said to Moises in the mount of Sinay hacedion or Hachedion And this name removeth wrath & sorrow and it encreaseth gladnes and love.

To Victory
Hoc est nomen q Adam in infernj circuitu &ᶜ

This is a name that Adam named in the environ of hell Mephenoyphaton. And who ever beareth it upon him any man shall not overcome him

Hæc sunt noia septem excelsa magna &ᶜ

These be the seven names great & virtuous when thou wylt axe any thing take thou a good hower and a good place. And els thou not hardy to name them. And these be the names Comiceton Sedelay. tohomos zofyn agata. bicol. ycos. It is ended. Do we thanks to our Lord Jesu Christ father and sonne and holy Amen, wᶜʰ liveth & reigneth wᵗʰout end Amen.

[58]

Incipit Canon libr: confectionis vel modus opandi &c
Heere beginneth the rule of the booke of consecration in the maner of worching.

In noie patris et fily et spus scti amen
filj mj p^{re}dilecte induere te vesti^{ts} &c
My son welbeloved Clothe thou thee wth new clothes and cleane wth wch was never vice nor synne ydone Be thou cleane sothely in soule and in body, thou shalt fast 9 dayes lenton fast standing praying devout and meeke solitary from earthly things and from fellowships sequestred, stable in the hope of God not doubting neither meaving. Saying everiche day of the nyne foresaid dayes the howers of rule of the day in his hower, and all good comon orisons that thou knowest And graces before meat and after forgett thou not, but wth huge effort and cleannesse of soule thou shalt say. And then sothely thou shalt have a booke of parchmyn of vellym that is Calves skynnes most cleane and most cleanly, of a cleane man written wth these nyne Orysons that is to witt (the first) *Deus invisibilis &c* The *second Deus uniuersi conditor*. The third *O gloriose adonay*. The 4th *On pie pn juste*. The 5th *Adonay melothe*. The 6th *omnipotens sempiterne deus*. The 7th *Pater de cælis*. The 8th *Osannu et æterna*. The 9th *In noie duj Jehu xpj* neither be there more written. Then go thou devoutly and divinely for to heare masse bearing wth thee the booke on Cleane syndall wrapped and when sothely the masse shall begynne or before putt thou the booke privily in a corner of the altar under the cloth where is said the holy gospel. And [58^v] so thou shalt heare the masse attentively and desyringly And manly thou shalt pray God that he vouchsafe to hallow this booke. And when the masse is done privily thou shalt take the booke and thou shalt come home wth booke eare that thou eate wch thure thou shalt ~~perfume~~ suffume all abouts wth water thou shalt spring wth holy water. And saying *Miserere mei deus* and so forth. And when thou hast done this putt it reverently upon a table wth sendell covered and made cleane in a chamber suffumed Then close thou it wth an holy stole (to the maner of a crosse after length thou shalt bynde) And wth ~~am~~ an holy girdle also of Latitude or bredth Then thou that long idle in words neither deeds hath bene bowing thy knees manly to the almighty thy face turned to the east say thou thy confession wth thilk versicles *Ne derelinquas me dne deus meus*. And when thou hast said these thou shalt say the 7 psalmes wth the letany in the end of wch thou shalt ad this forme (*ut tu deus oipus &c*) And when thou hast said this thou shalt open thy booke and in the opening thou shalt say *Deus*

Miserere mei. And when thy booke is open say thy confession wth the versicles as rather thou didst. And when thou hast ended say meekly and hartily this Orison *benedicat te pater &^c* And it behoveth to do no more that day. And this same by nyne dayes shall be used And when w^thout doubt this booke shall be had [59] Consecrate or ha[llow]ed.[1] And wth this booke thus Consecrate after thou might hallowe many other that they have strength and effect, after thy desyer and the rule of thy art, and thou shalt come to the end covered when sothely thou wilt hallow exp^erim^te or invocationes only or of eche other togither If in the first maner thus thou shalt hallow: put thou thilke exp^erim^te upon a cleane table covered wth cleane sendell in the rather house, that is in a cleane chamber and honest Then thy face turned to the east thy knees bowed to the Almighty say thy confiteor wth the forsaid versicles that is to wytt *Ne derelinquas me dne Deus meus.* And when thou hast said these say this Orison *Deus invisibilis* And when thou hast said it say thy Confiteor wth the foresaid versicles. Afterward say *Deus universi conditor.* And when this is ended say thy confiteor wth the versicle. Afterward *O gloriose Adonay* And when it is said, say thy Confiteor wth the versicle Afterward say *Adonay meloth &^c* And thus thou shalt do by 3 dayes everiche day 3 or 4 tymes that is in the morning in the midday in the eventide and at midnight. And if thou mayst not so ofte, at least say it at morning and at even ne leave out not And knowe thou that in thilk orison. In the role consecrate i in c p^ropocionis thou shalt number thy peticions and thou shalt change for thy will and need. That is thou shalt keepe for thilke place where it is [59^V] said in aire potestates &^c till there per scti ssimu nomen tuu. If in the second maner then thou shalt say by order as thou shalt do in the first netheles not changing thy peticion but as it is in thy head saying. And when thou hast done this thou shalt say thy confiteor wth the versicle. And when thou hast said this say this Orison *Omps sempiterne deus.* And when thou hast said this say thy confiteor wth the versicle beforesaid After ward say *Pater de cælis* And when thou hast said this say *Osanna et æterna.* And then say thy Confiteor wth the versicle before Jesu xpc &^c And when thou hast done this By 3 dayes as aforesaid it shall be well made sure and stable w^thout doubt Wherfore heere be taken invocacons generally for books what ever they be where spirits be incleped, either for exp^erim^te where they be above cleped, wch by another man be named Questions, exercizations vincula or bonds &^c ffurthermore knowe thou that this Orison *In noie dni nri &^c* avayleth to this that is said. And also avayleth to op^eracon or worching. ffor when a man worcheth in art or in deed he ought to say thus and to p^reconize or this ought to be said and p^reconized. But in the third maner do thou fully as it is said in the second maner. ffor if thou put

---

[1] Smudged between brackets.

under the Coniunction the coniuncti ff peticion of the first maner togither
and of the second so in the same [60] maner thou shalt have. And if any man
may not do this neither his worke or intent to effect (led by such maner
doctrine) eche man then cease & distreyne ffor sothely I say that he who ever
it be thus cannot have himself as the rule of this book enformeth neither he
can or knoweth that this is worse and most letting of his synnes, or
p^eradventure he will not amend himself (as it accordeth) what wonder thou
therefore if such ones feele impedim^lt or letting. Therfor blessed be he that
these might holily & spedefully diffinishe. And knowe thou that when ever
thou saist thy Confiteor Then anon after thou shalt sprinkle thee wth holy
water and wth the signe if the holy crosse signe thee
Heere endeth the Canon or Rule

And heereafter beginneth thorisons for to hallow the book wth meeke
devocion & wth all theffect or desire of the harte say thou *Ut tu Deus ompo
omnia et bonitate tua sctifices et benedicas et Consecres lib istu sctissimis nuibz tuis
insignitu vt virutute quæ obtinere debut potenter obtiveat vz ad Conservand vincta
spm et omnes invocationes et Coniurationes ipor et oia etiam alia quemlt exp^erimenta
vel bria vel instrumenta seu quæg alia &^c*

*Deus ms Miserere mei et p^rce malis meis sana aiam mea quia peccavi non abneges
vni quod plurbus contulisti Exandi Deus Orationem famuli tui ut in quocunq die
invocaveio te velocity exandi me sicut exandisti Maria Magdelana Suscipe domine
[60^V] Clamore confitentis Exandi Due voce p^rcantis et p. oratione beatissimæ
virginis Mariæ matris tuæ atq oium sctor tuo el orones et p^rces perveniat ad aures
piotatis tuæ quas ego N p^r. hoc libro Consecrando effundo cora te in hac hora ut p.
tua sctissima noia quæ in ipso continent^or sit consecratus et confirmatus ad
quodcunq volnero p^rstante duo nro Jesu xpo qui vivit et regnat Deus p. Aia secula
seculor*

*Due Jesu xpe fili dei vivi p. ineffabile miam tua p.^ce mihi et Miserere mei et exandi
me ome p. invocatione nois trinitatis S. S. P.ris et filij et spus scti acceptas habeas et
placeant tibi orones et verba oris mei p. invocatione tuor sctor noius in hoc libro
scriptor humiliter et fideliter depcanes licet ego N indignus tamen in te confidens ut
sctifices et benedicas libr istu tuis sctissima noia ss On Jesus xpus Alpha et Ω el ely
eloy eloye onoytheon stimulamaton alzephares tetragrammaton eliora egiron
ynsirion oristion orconay usiormis vel usior ormis one labiazin Noyn. Messya sother
emanuel sabaoth adonay et p. oia secreta noia tua quæ non licet hoi loqui et p. hæc
noia quæ in hoc libro continent^r et p. et potestate tua divina sit liber iste consecratus
+ benedctus + snaguinis tui ut virtute qua debet et desidero obtinere obtineat et
veraciter sine aliqua [61^R] fallacia et efficaciter valeat ad consecrandu vincula spm et*

oia experim^{ta} *to*^r *ta et invocationes et coniurationes spiu et bria portabit signa figura et charact*^r *et quæq alia volnero ut sctam virtute et potestatem obtineant et habeant p. p*^{er}*puo ad quælibt ad quæ illa sunt constituta p*^r*stante duo qui sedet in altissimis cui honor et Gloria in secula seculor Amen.*

Benedicat te + pater benedicat te + filius benedicat te + spus sctus scta mater dui nri Jesu p.pi te benedicat + et sanctificet + ut vitute sacri in te N obtineat quæ obitnere debes benedicant te + æs sctæ virgines benedicant te + hodie et omni tempore æs scti et electi æs virtutes Cælestes te + benedi cant et Confirment æs Angeli et Archangeli æs virtutes Dei principatus et potestates throni duaciones Cherubin et serafin ex authoritate et licentia Dei te + benedicant p. merita et orones et invocationes omn sctor tuor due Jesu p.pe benedicas + sanctifices + et consernes + libr P. et confirmes + p. oipotentia tua et virtute et potestate obtineat ad qua constitutus est et confirmes p^r*stante duo nro Jhesu p.po cuius regnu et inp.in sine fine p.manet in sæcula sæculor Amen*

These be the versicles that should be said after the Confiteor

Ne derelinquas me due Deus meus ne discesseris a me intende in auditorin men due salutis meæ fiat mia tua due sup. Nos quemadmodu speravimus in to In te due speravi non Confundar in æternu Intret in Conspectu tuo oro mea due et inclina auræ tua ad p^r *ces meas Due exandi orone mea et clamor meus ad te veniat deus potentissime Deus sctissime fortissime*

Liber Lunæ

Heere beginneth thorisons that ought to be written in the booke consecrate

The first Orison   *Oro prima*

Deus Invisibilus, Deus inestimabilis, Deus ineffabilis Deus incommutabilis, Deus incorruptibilis, Deus piissime Deus dulcissime, Deus excelse, deus gloriose Deus immense, Deus totius miæ Ego N. Licot indignus plenus iniquitate dolo et malitia supplex ad tua vera venio miam orans et deprecans ut non respicias ad universa et innumerabilia peccata mea sed sicut consuevisti peccator misereri et preces humiliu exandire, ita me famulu tuu N. licet in dignu exandire digneris clamante ad tex hoc expᵉʳimᵗᵒ sctissimis noibus tuis insignito, ut virtute obtineat S. æreas potestates et infernales princepes pᵉʳ hane orone consecrate mirabil constringat ut velint nolint humanæ voluntati obediant et cum exorcizator voluerit æs ad um congerget et cum vluerit disperget pᵉʳ sctissimu nomen tuu q quatuor literis scribitᵒʳ Ioth theos agla yaym deus eloy quo audito mane retrogradit ᵒʳ ois ær conculcatᵒʳ terra tremit ignis extinguitᵒʳ ois quoq cælestis exercitus tremit et infernalis tremit et turbatᵒʳ et pᵉʳ hæc sctissima noia On alpha et Ω principiu et finis el ely elœ eloy Elyon sother emanuel sabaoth adonay egge ya ya ye ye consecratᵒʳ hoc expᵉʳimᵗᵘ deo pʳᵉstante qui sedet in altissimis cui laus est et Gloria atg honor pᵉʳ infinita secula Amen

If sothely thou wilt hallow any expᵉʳimᵗ that pᵉʳtayneth not to invocation of spirits then thou shalt say thus *me exandire digneris* [62] *clamante ad te pᵉʳ hoc expᵉʳimᵗᵉ vy virtute quam obtinere debet potenter habeat et obtineat pᵉʳ sctissimu nomen tnu q scribitᵒʳ in isto libro*

The second Orison

Deus universi conditor orbis qui Cælu supᵉʳ nubiu altitudine extendisti et terra in sua stabilitatefundasti et mari terminu suu quem pᵉʳterire no potest tribnisti qui solem et Luna et stellas in sumo ære collocasti qui oia in sepia fecisti qui sexton die hoiem ad imagine tua plasmasti que et cu Eva propter mandate tui prevaricatione de paradise pᵉʳiecisti qui genus humnai in aqua diluvii perdidisti qui Noe et æs qui cu eo errant im archa salvasti. Qui Abrahæ sub triplici persona ad radice mambre apparnisti Qui Loth de submersione Gomorrhæ et Sodomæ liberasti. Qui Moysi in medio Pubi in flama ignus locutus fnisti. Qui populu tuu de Captivitate Egipti eduxisti et ei pᵉʳ mediu mare via apernisti. Qui lege Moysi in monte Sinay dedisti Qui de petra aquas manare fecisti. Qui Daniele de Lacu leonu eripnisti Qui tres pneros de camino ignis ardentis S. Sidrach Misach et Abednago illæsos abire fecisti. Qui Susanna in te Confidente de falso crimine liberasti. Qui Jona propheta in ventre ceti salvasti pᵉʳ hæc multa et alia miracula quæ fecisti exandi pʳᵒpitious pie. Jesu *orone famuli tui N. et da huic exp*er*im*te *virtute et potestate super malignos spus ad congregandu ipsos et ad slvemen et ad ligandu et ad maledicendu et in profundu abysti p*er*ijciendu si non obedierint exorcizatori, duo p*ro*sante qui sctus benedictus regnat p*er oia secula seculor Amen.*

[62ᵛ]

The third Orison

*Oh gloriose Adonay p*er *que creant*or *oia regunt*or *et consistent adesto perpitius invocationibus meis et clementer p*re*sta ut hoc exp*er*im*te *p Deu virtute et potestatem obtineat ad subingandu malignos spus ut velint nolint exorcizatori humiliter obediant et mandata eius adimpleant te invante et inbente qui sedes in altissimis et cuncta custodis cui sit honor et potestas p*er *infinita secula seculor Amen*

The fourth Orison

*On pie on Juste Adonay sctissim*e *qui misericordiæet pietatis es origo Rex regn et dus duantin qui sedes in mæistate tua intueris profundu abyssi omnia cernens oia regens oia pugillo continens qui virtute tua cumtis moderaris qui hoiem ad imagine et similitudine tua de limo terræ formasti, ut sic in terra landeris et glorificoris sicut in Cælo et omnis terra adoret te deus et psallat libi et ego N. licet indignus psalum dicam noi tuo altissimo, unde pijssime et misericordissime Deus maiestate tua imploro et cu humili devotione suppliciter exposco ut in virtute tua et dono græ tuæ consecrent*or *et confirment*or *orone et consecrationes quæ in hoc scribnut*or *ut virtute et effcacia ad qua institutæ sunt potenter obtineant et potestatem exorcizatori super malignos spus perfecte tribant ut cu p*er *ipsum et p*er *ipsas invocati et exorcizati fuerint statim ex oi parte conveniant et response veraciter et recte reddant et mandata exorcizatoris cito et efficaciter proficient illo p*er*stante* [63] *cui laus est et potestas qui etiam regnat et imperat p*er *æterna secula seculor Amen*

The fifth Orison

*Adonay Meloth Adonay Auboth beola Nathath Adonay in quo oia Creata et sctificata sunt misericordia tua et ineffablie pietate tua p*er *hæc santissima noia invoco te ut mihi postulanti licet indigno famulo tuo N. auxiliu græ tuæ p*r*stare digneris super has orones consecrationes et invocationes tuis sctissimis noibus insignitis quæ in hoc libro continent*or *S. on el eloe Adonay Saday alpha et Ω yaheyhe hassery usion panton craton tetragrammaton elzephares occmomos vel occmomoy anoy theon stimilmaton on. ely elion ely eloy eliora messias sother emanuel sabaoth pantather panteon pancraton premellius principiu primogenitus sapiam uertes cralathon splendor Gloria lux panis fons vitis mons hostin Ianna petra lapis es verbu salus angelus sponsus leo vermis athanathos kiros agiros otheos p*er *hæc sctissima noia et p*er *alia quæ noiare non licet te suppliciter expostulo ut orationibus et consecrationibus atg invocationibus istis quæ continent*or *in hoc libro virtutem et* *potestate tribnas p^{er} virtute tua divina ad consecrandu oia exp^{er}imenta et invocationes demonu ut ubicunq maligni spus in virtute tuor nuuim fuerit adiurati et exorcizatoris* ~~dileng~~ *diligenter adimpleat ut nihil sint nocentes neg terrore inferentes sed potius obedientas et ministrantes et tua districti virtute mandata proficient fiat fiat fiat Amen*

Knowe thou that if thou wilt compound or make any exp^{er}imt of new to thy pleasure or liking put [63^V] to it this teaching. Hoc est talem virtute vel talem vim &^{c} That is such vertue or such strength &^{c} and hallow thou it as it is aforesaid and it shall consecrate that thou come to effort or speed.

Heere beginneth the generall consecration of spirits for to gett downe power for to clepe thilk spirits to bynde to lose to comannd to curse and to confound or washe. ffor to hallow exp^{er}imt^e say thou hither But for to hallow bonds & other say thou

The sixth Orison

Omnipotens semperiterne Deus qui in principio Cuncta ex nihilo creasti cui obediant œs creaturæ cui œ genu flectit^{or} cælestiu terrestriu et infernor quem tremuit angeli et archangeli tui duationes et potestates adorant et tremuit qui manu clandis oia et Adam ad similitudine tuam fecesti et angelos tuos incredulous p^{er} superbia eor in profundu tartari oiecisti te rogo et peto clemetissime pater oipx et obsecro to p^{er} Ihm xpm filiu tuu in cuins ptate sunt oia qui sedet ad dextra tua pater oips qui venturus est indicare vivos et mortuos et seculu p^{er} igne quaternus tu Deus Ihu ppe qui es Alpha et Ω primus et novissimus Rex regu dus duantiu loth agla sabaoth et abiel onathi anathæl amaziel gudoniel agios chelias ylkiros anathanatos ymas ely messiah p^{er} hæc tua noia et p^{er} oia alia advoco te et obsecro te p^{er} nativitate tua Jesu ppe p^{er} pueru pannis involutu p^{er} baptisum tuu et p^{er} passione tua et p^{er} resurrectione tua et p^{er} ascencione tuæ, et p^{er} spm sctm p^{er}acletu [64] p^{er} amarityudine aiæ tuæ qu exivit de corpore et p^{er} quinq vulnera tua et per mortem tua et p^{er} sanguine et aqua quæ exivernut de corpore tuo p^{er} misericorda et oiptentia tua et virtute ineffabile tua et p^{er} sacram^{tu} q dedisti discipulis tuis pride antequa fuisti passus, et p^{er} sctam trinitate individual p^{er} prophetas et patriarchas et p^{er} œs sctos tuos et scats tuas et p^{er} oia sacra mysteria et beneficia quæ sunt in honore tuo et p^{er} sctissima noia tua cognita et incognita adoro te et invoco te obsecro et benedico te et rotœ ut acceptas habeas onones et consecrationes et verba oris mei quibus utor Peto Deus oips virtute et potestate super œs angelos tuos qui de cælo eiecti sunt decipientes genus humanu ad loquela eor abstrahendu ad constringendu eos eoram me et ad percipiendu eis oia quæ eis facere sunt possibilia, et ne me verbamea voce mea ullo modo contemnant sed mihi et dictis meis simper obediant el nide timeant. P^{er} humilitat^e miam tua et gratia tua deprecor et peto te p^{er} oia noia tua Athon arathon uegethon ya – yraien knemnoy *usion: ysilosi et p^er œs sctus et scats et p^er angelus et archangelos potestates duationes et virtutes et p^er istue nomen p^er q Salonon constringebat demones et conculstieos S. Booth hebant heth agla Joth oths Sabaoth phanabaoth et p^er virtutem eorunde quatemis me petente congregare et consstringere eos concedas ut nihi rudeant corporis et aiæ [64^V] p^er dum nrm Jhm p^erpm filiu tuu qui vivis et regnas Deus in vintate scti spus p^er oia secula seculor Amen*

Pater de cælis deus unus un substantia trinitas in p^ersonis qui Ada et Eva et plurimos alios parcari permisisti et ti x peccatis eor crucifigi et mori sustinnisti clementissinne pater te q. peto et rogo supplex niodis oibus quibus possu p^er alpha et Ω xpm filin tuu ut me N congregare et coandunare permittas angelos tuos quondam incredulous qui habent poteste nihi alloqui et facere quæ volo et desydero sinelæsione alicnius et nocumento p^orsta et principne dedisti virtute lapidis herbar verbor et noium tuor nobis potestate ligandi solvendi demones verbis nris et anxilio tuo q concedas permirar bilem virtute tua p^er oipotentia Amen

O suma et æterna deitas et virtus altissima qui te dispot his vero indicio vocaris noibus Onoytheon Elzephares Tetragramaton stimulamaTon Eloyoram Egiron usirion oristion oriona usiormis vel usionia onelga braysyn neym Joseph messias sother Emanuel Sabaoth adonay Te invoco te adoro te totis viribus mentis implore quatenus p^er te putes orationes consecrationes et invocacœs in hoc libro existents consecrent^or et p^reparent^or quemadmodu convenit . s. ubicunq maligni spus in virtute tuor noin fuerint invocati et exorcizati statim ex oi parte conveniant et non smt nocentes neq terrore inferentes sed potius obedientes et ministrantes et tua [65] districti virtute mandata exercizatoris perficiant Amen

In noie dni nri Jhu xpi patris et f et s.s. scta trinitas et inseperabilis unitas te invoco us ss mihi salus defensio et protection corporis et animæ meæ mmc et imp^erpm p^er virtute crucis et passionetua dep^reco rte Due nr Jesu xpe fili dei vivi p^er merita et intercessiones beatissimæ matris tuæ Mariæ et oinm sctor sctar[ ]q^1 tuar ut mihi concedas gram tua et pietate slr et potestate diam super œs malignos spus ut quotiescunq virutue tuor noium eos invocavero statim ex oi parte conveniant et voluntate mea perfecte adimpleant q nihil sint nocentes sed potius obedientes p^er et ministrants et tua districti virtute mandata mea perficiant Amen

Explicit

---

[1] A smudge here between the brackets.

Liber Lunæ

Cum volneris subscribbere ad oiu aspice solem &c When thou wilt write to hate behold thou the sonne and the day of him ffor if thou fyndest it in ♈ ♌ or ♐ worke thou to hate in the first hower of the same for it is the hower of solis. And write thou the name of the day and the name of the hower and the Charact of Solis wᶜʰ be thend of this booke nempning the separation or departing betwixt everich either pᵉʳson seethe this scripture is full necessary And if it befalleth that ♂ be wᵗʰ ☉ it shall be stronger to this that thou wilt worche And work thou not but if ☉ be in fiery signes And worke thou nothing in other howers of the same day.

The day of Luna the first hower of same is to write in it Þ to entering upon kings and axe thy things and change thou what things thou wylte. And be thou warefor the coming betweene of Luna to Caput draconis that is in the first knott fro it is secret & hid Also when it cometh to the second knott and the third And be thou ware from other knottes if sothely thou wilt worke to payne & perdition worke thou by the fowre last knottes. And when Luna were in any of these thy worke shall be fulfilled in thine axing. And the viᵗʰ hower of the day of Luna in veneris. Therfore worke thou in it to love and the viiᵗʰ of the same is of ☿ worke thou in it to dilection of men togither. And the day of Luna accordeth generally to eache worke that thou wilt And most if Luna were in ♉ or ♋ or ♓ And if ♀ were wᵗʰ it thy worke shall be stronger and it shall helpe to suffer betwixt the man and the woman Therfore worke thou all these on diminution of Luna The day of ♂ the first hower of it when therefore thou wilt make sicke any man or woman wᵗʰ divers torments in bynding or losing of body or taking away of wytt or what ever thou wilt any man suffer in his body thy work shall be fulfilled and thou shalt fulfill in it Therfore dread thou God and let not a true man and worke thou in the first hower of the day of ♂ and write what thou wilt. After that thou hast written the name of the man & the name [66] of the day and the name of the hower and the name of ♂ and write thou the characts of ♂ and wᵗʰ all this thou shalt fulfill The second hower of it is of ☉ worke thou in it like to this when ☉ werein his fiery signes And write thou the names as I have beforesaid to the characts of ☉ and the name And if ♂ were in ♏ bynde thou serpents & scorpions. And the third hower is of ♀ worke thou in it to all love when he were in his fortune or exaltation for then it shall be sharper in this thing. Thou shalt write the name of the hower of it and of the day and the characts of it for thou shalt profitt. And the 4ᵗʰ hower is of ☿ write in it to hate and departing and thou shalt write the characts of ☿ and the names as it is said in other planets The day of ☿ the first hower os if it of wᶜʰ the empire is strong when it were in his exaltation worke thou in the hower of privy things. And the 2 hower is of ☽ write thou in it to peticions of ☿ And worke thou not in other howers of this day any thing. The day of ♃ the first hower of it is write Þ in it To kings and enter thou upon them when ♃ were in   [1]   And bynde thou shippes that were in the sea And if ☽ were wth it, it shall be stronger in all things that thou shalt worke in kings and of other & to concord betweene them that be attwayne And worke thou in it to love of women when he were in his fortune. And write the names & characts after that I have before said to thee And the 2 hower is of ☿ write & afflicttion of him that thou wylt. And the 3 is of ☽ worke thou in it to divers & all things that thou wilt.

[66^V]

The day of ♄ the first hower of it is worke thou in it to all odible works betweene friends, do all worke that thou wilt in the same hower of waxe and Lute. And if thou wilt make a man sicke take of the clothes of him if thou might & write in them the working of the man& the name of the hower, & the name of the day. and cast into a fyer that is not quenched as the fier of a bath & of and oven and this shall be the sicknes of him. And if then ♄ were in his fortune or in his exaltation the worke of him shall be stronger. The first hower the name of it is *hebiem* the second *luuer*. The third *Camu*. The fourth *telgilim* the fifth *Tathalit*. The sixth *Tenhor*. The 7th *Jador*. The 8th *Jafatu*. The 9th *Baron* The 10th *Jahon*. The 11th *Jebron*. The 12th *aliachalon*. In the first hower is made orison of men to their God It is good in it to bynde all tongs In the second is made the orisons of angells to the Lord and in the same be made works of concord or dilection or love betweene men and to all creatures of eache spirit. In the third fowles bringeth thankings to their Lord In it be made the works of fowles and of fishes In the 4th creatures do thankings to their Lord In it be made the works of serpents & of scorpions. In the 5th eache beast doth thankings to the Lord In it be made the workes of wolves & of wilde beasts fowre footed In the 6th is made the orison of Cherubin to their Lord for [67] encreasing of all things and of incantations And in it be made the works of them that is p^risoned and they be delivered. In the 7th is made the orison of them that fasteneth the throne. In the 8 be made the workings of dep^artings & strife beside creatures. In the 9th be made the workings of taveling men that theeves lett them not neither go out to them w^thout end. In the 10th waters singeth to their lord and in yt descendeth the spirit of the Lord and he maketh to tremble, and the worke of taking of kings be made and entring to them, and they should not speake to him evill. And if water

---

[1] There is a space in the manuscript here.

were taken in yt and were medled to an oyntm^t made holy or hallowed and wth this he were annoynted that suffereth spasmu it shall p^{ro}fitt to him bythe comanndemt of God almighty. In the xith just men be glad. And in it be made the works of love and of concord. In the xiith men be outcast and in it be made the works of sylence that they speake not furthermore upon whome they be made.

Si quis maxima dilectionis reverentiæ et benignitatis &^{c}
Who ever willeth himself to be seene and be had of most dilection reverence & benignity in the hower of ♃ in the day of him ☉ be it fused of brasse and that most privily and wth cleannesse and grave he his name in ☉ wch avoideth wth the ayre, and wth good odo^{r}s be it filled. And this orison among there ne leave he not *O Jou fulgentissimu sps neg in honore et dilectione populi et maxima poteste sublevate corda potehntu voluntates* [67^v] *hoinm meæ voluntati convenire,* And when that is done be it wrapped in cleane clothes and in the Cloth be paynted the seale of Jovis And in the middle of the city in wch he willeth to be, be it burned. If sothely thou wilt make concord make ☉ in the howre of Jou or of some lving Joue, and one clepe that other and be it put Under the earth togither. And the foresaid orison Be it not leaved or be it not still for any love added If sothely any man would be holden wth the love of any woman make he ☉ in the hower of ♃ and in his day and o[?]^{1}of him in the hower of ♀ or be it ^{2} or be it paynted in most cleane and white p^{ar}chement. And his name in the head of the planet and in the brest, and that one kisse that other and clepe. And about the head seales of the planets be they paynted, And when this is done be they suffumed wth thure & croco and in the hower of action this orison be it not leaved *O Jovis et Veneris amabiles et grales sps amore .S. cordi illius adtubete sup ☉ meam cordi ejus imprimite ut quandiu res ista duraverit se mitri ad voluntate mra exhibeat potentiaq creatoris.* And then if it be metall in the responsory of this to wch it is direct be they putt under the earth if paynted upon him to whome the love neded & besides the beholding of him for whome it was made.

---

^{1} Unclear script here.
^{2} There is a space in the manuscripts here.

[68]

Dixit Thebit Pencorat dixit ar[h1] *qui legerit &*[c]

Thebit Pencorat said Ar[h] said who that readeth Philsophy and geometry and all science & were alien from Astronomy ffor it is more p[re]cious then Geometry and higher then Philosophy. It is more imaginative science. Ar[h] the pher[2] said in the third treatise of his booke de anima that is of the soule ffor as a body is not moved that lacketh the soule or lyfe neither lyfe is to the soule but by meate w[th] w[ch] the natures of him be disfyed so they lacketh light of wisdome and of science when they be made wyde of Astronomy. And ad the soule or lyfe may not stande but by meate by whome natures of the bodyes be disfyed, also nature is the roote of wisdome anents him that lacketh astronomy neither there is a light of Geometry when he would voyd from Astronomy. And astronomy is more p[re]cious and higher then all science.

Thebit said when thou wilt any thing of all things Of worke Know thou ~~that~~ that Philosophers have comended to us in fer reposacle 7 works w[ch]we useth in each maner w[ch] were p[ro]fitt p[ro]vocation or expulsion of ympediment. And now I have shewed before to thee in my booke chapters. And I have put them for similitude or likenesse w[th] w[ch] it is worke of some worke for to chase away scorpions When thou wilt worke thou shalt begin under Ascension of Scorpius and thou shalt figure ☉ of a scorpion of brasse or tynne ot lead or sylver or gold and thou shalt grave upon ☉ the name of the Ascendent and the Lord of him and the Lord of the day and the Lord of thehower and the name of Luna, and Luna be it in Scorpius. And thou shalt make the Ascendent infortunate as thou might better and [68[v]] the Lord of the Ascendent and thou shalt make the house of ♂ infortunate, and thou shalt put in the house of ♂ or be it Joyned to evill in the 4th or in the 5th or in the 7th. And when thou hast done this thou shalt put under the earth or bury the head downeward and thou shalt say in the hower of the sepulture of it *Hæc est Sepultura ejus N vt non ingrediatur locu istu N* and that he enter not into this place N. And thou shalt bury it in the middle of the place from wch thou wilt that be taken away from it or in the place of the dwelling of him or in the place[3]of conversation of him. And if thou maketh 4 ☉ after this disposition and burneth everich in each quarter of them of the quarters of the place from w[ch] thou wilt them to be taken away it shall be more profitable & better. Also do thou all thing that thou wilt of all maner of beasts letting

---

[1] Aristotle.

[2] Philosopher.

[3] In the margin here: plates . O.

when thou wylt put them out and begin thou this under the Ascension of like kynde of them wch thou wilt put out or do away. Also do thou when thou wilt destroy a region or let it. make ☉ under the Ascension of that city, and thou shalt make infortunate the Lord of the house of Death. And thou shalt make infortunate the Lord of the Ascendent and Luna and the house of Luna. And thou shalt make infortunate the xth house if thou might & bury thou ☉ in the midst of it, anfd thoushalt see wonderfull things of marvels. Also when thou wilt let any man d othou lyke to this worke and be it not fortunate in any thing how long ☉ were in the place [69] of it the will of God y keepe

Cum volueris extruere domu regione &^c
When thou wilt shape any house region or city or place the places use thou fortunes or thous shalt putt fortune on thascendent of it andin the 10th or in the xi^th or in the viii^th And thou shalt make fortunate the Lord of thascendent And the Lord of the house pf thascendent. Thou shalt make fortunate Luna and the Lord of the house of him is thou hast done by these that be evill and thou shalt see wonderfull things.

Quida destruxit regnu hoc modo &^c
Some man destroyed a realme in his maner. He made infortunate the Ascendent of the region & the Lord of him and the Lord of the Ascendent. And he made ♄ infortunate and he putt him the Lord of the hower, and he hid the fortunes that is, he made them to be absent from the ascendant And the Lord of him And he made the fortunes to fall from triplicy of the ascendant and from the corners And he wrote in ☉ the name of the region, and the name of the ascendant and the Lord of him and the name of the Lord of the hower and the name of the Lord of the day and thr p^arty of evils & the Lord of him and the Lord of the signe in the wch the wall fill. And he buryed ☉ in the middle of the region. And he putt w^thin ☉ of the earth of the region of the 4 quarters of yt East west north and south And he said in the sepulchre this ☉ be made of destruction of the place N When thou wilt make ☉ that asketh substannce that is taken be strength from him or denyed or letted and thou wylte that it be holden to him make to him ☉ of [69^v] gold or silver or brasse or of them wch it might be made. And begin thou to worke under thascension of Interrogation of him. And make thou the Lord of the house of him to be under ioyned wth the Lord of thascendent, and be there betwixt them receiving, and the coniunction of them, be it from the third or the vi^th beholding. And it accordeth that the Lord of the house of substannce be in signes obeying and the Lord of thascendent in signes comannding this sothely shall be stronger and the signes obeying to them crooked or bowed

and they that comanndeth be they direct or even. And thou shalt make fortunate the ascendant and the Lord of him. And beware least the Lord of thascendent be retrograde or combust or falling or of his opposition, that is of his 7th house lest he be letted of evill, but be he stronger in the corner. And thou shalt make fortunate the ascendant, and the Lord of the substance and Luna. And when thou hast made them after this disposition thou shalt keepe it. And then converted thou shalt make another ☉ wch shall be signifier anents whome shall be the substannce of it were anents a kyng The second ☉ or worching begin it under the 10 from the ascendant first, and if it were anents a prince, or a friend or a theefe or the contrary or other such begin thou the second ☉ under such an ascendant that it pertayne to him anents whome it is [70] hoped the substannce to be that is if it were anentis the sonne do under the 5th if anentis the father under the 4th also under the signes after as it appertaineth to him, and put thou either strong & fortunate wthout imedimt. And put thou the question of him wth it of the third or sixt beholding And put the significator of him to whome thou makest that is the signification of the second ☉ Joyned wth the Lord of the first ascendant and he shall receive him and make thou all evill falling from him And thou shalt make fortunate thre 10 and the 4 if thou might or some of them wch nevertheless were profit of wch the first. Put thou the face of one towards the face of another and wrappe thou either in a cleane sloth and bury thou them in the middle of the house of the enquirer or searcher under a signe fortunate wth strong fortunes And turne the face of ☉ when thou buriest it toward the North And if the enquirer were much going that is if he be oft moved from place to place and it be joyned to him anentis whome the substance were put thou ever either ☉es or worchings wth him that he beare them wth him where ever he go. And knowe thou that when thou hast done this and hath wrought wisely the worchings after that as I have aforesaid to thee, thou shalt fynde that thou hast sought substannce searcheth not of any man any thing, but he will that the chaffer of him increase and the wynning of him be multiplyed, that is, he accordeth [70v] and his wytt is dressed and maiest that lightly he fynde his liflood and the things wch be necessary make to him ☉ of negotiation or of merchandize and begin to worche under thascendent of the nativity of him if thou knowest it, or under the ascension of his interrogation. And thou shalt forme thascendent and the Lord of him & Luna and the Lord of the house of him. And the 10 and the Lord of him. Luna sothely and the Lord of the house of him, and make thou the Lord of the second houseto be ioyned wth the Lord of thascendent of the third or sixt beholding And be there betwixt them receiving that the planet be in the house of the planet to wch it is Joyned or in exaltation of it And thou shalt fortune the 11 and the

Lord of him and the 8[1] if thou might and put thou the party of the fortune in thascendent or in the 10. And when thou hast done most certainly under theis Constellation or condition The Lord of this shall not cease how long the ☉ were kept wᵗʰ him to kepe get substance in things hoped and unhoped And if he knoweth himself need errand or maistry or in any worke he shall get them and lightly he shall do his vowe and they be made to him and he shall have concord and winnings in his errands or in deeds till thou see in getting of his liflood that he desireth and thing cometh to him wᵗʰout travell & he shall [71] be fortunate in adquisition or purchasing or getting The third part of principall and domes the worke of ☉ to him that would be before to a city or to any region of the king when thou wilt. This thou shalt begynne ffirst to take interrogation most certaine of it wᵗʰ radicall intention whether be shall be before to that place or no wᶜʰ he axeth. And when it appeareth to thee of signification of the ascentdent that he shall be before and that thilke prelation shall be in the same yeere Thy worke shall be sooth and it shall be fulfilled If sothely thy axing signifyeth that it is not neither shall be fulfilled in that yeere, neither do thou to it any thing in the same yeere till the yeere of it be revolved or overturned And thou shalt make a roote most very and before shewed And also these thou shallt do in eche worke that thou shalt do if eche kynde thou shalt behold into theffect and harme of it. And when the significators have signified effect or speed worke thou the working to this that they signifyeth to worke If sothely the significatoʳˢ signifyeth harme Do that thou wilt of the working that were to destroy for the most true shall appeare to hit And beware least thou make thy working of destruction under interrogacon thascendent of wᶜʰ signifyeth effect. When therefore thou wilt make ☉ or worching to him that willeth to be before to a city or to a region or to any principate on eworke sothely is in all these ffirst thou shalt shape the forme in wᶜʰ thou shalt fuse of hold ☉ grave thou therefore the head of ☉ under the Ascension of Caput draconis [71ⱽ] And the being of the Lord of thascendent be it good and be it free from evils and thou shalt grave the body of ☉ under the ascension in wᶜʰ ☽ were and Luna be it increased of light and ioyned to a planet of fortune And thou shalt grave sothely the shoulders and the brest under thascension in wᶜʰ ♃ were. And thou shalt grave the wombe inder the ascension in wᶜʰ ♀ were. And the haunches under the ascension in wᶜʰ is Sol. And Sol be it in his dignityes, and the lyenes under thascension in wᶜʰ be ♀ not retrograde neither combust but be it free from evill and be it in some dignities fortunate and formed. After grave thou the feete under the Ascension in wᶜʰ were Luna and ☽ being ioyned wᵗʰ ♀

---

[1] Not sure of this.

And when thou hast made wisely the forme Thou shalt begin to make ☉ of a man holding in the forme if thou wilt of gold or of silver or of lead or of brasse or tynne, and charge thou not of wch of the mettalls it were. Or that thou make it sothely health or strength in thascension Onely is to be sought Begin thou therfore to make ☉ under the ascension of the nativity of him if thou knowest this or under the ascension of interrogacon or axing of it. And thou shalt name ☉ by his name knowen or open, and thou shalt make fortunate thascendent and the 10 and the Lord of thascendent And thou shalt make the evill absent from thascendent and the Lord of him And thou shalt put the 11 Lord a planett fortunate Beholding the ascendant wch frendful beholding [72] of coniunction and receive he him wth p^erfect receiving for then thou hast done and fulfilled ☉ or working after this maner and it were p^erfect to thee shall be gotten that he axed of his king, and he shall wynne the principality and that he axeth keep therefore that I have before said and thou shalt profitt if God will. And these workings may be exercised in love and hate if he that exerciseth seeth well the higher meavings, that is if he knowe well the courses of planetts, and other things that to this profiteth when thou p^roposed zegim councell or question or ☉ to Inclination or bowing of a kyng against any of his men, and councello^rs that he be bowed to him that is wth his dilection or love, and the place of him be raised anenst him that is that he be hono^red of him when thou wilt do thou shalt beginne first to take it a very ascension, after this thou shalt behold where there be betwixt the Lord of thascendent ioyned to the 10 lored of the 3 or vi^th beholding, and there were betwixt them p^erfect receiving and there were good being of both, and both were free from evils and thou findest the Lord in thascendent 10 beholding the ascendant the thing sothely shall be fulfilled and the worching shall be very or soothe If sothely thou fyndest nothing of these wch I have said but thou findest thascendent and the 10 from evils the thing shall be fulfilled, and the worching shall be very or soothe, and a great trace shall appeare If sothely thou fyndest the Lord of the 10 letted in other [72^V] letting and the Lord of the ascendant or ascendants and thous fyndest nothing of these that I have said Ne do thou not to them any thing for that is begon shall not be fulfilled. If sothely the interrogation signifyeth theffect abd thou wyly do the ☉ or worchinh begin thou to do after as I have disposed in the graving of the forme wth that condicion that I have before said to thee Grave thou ☉ of a man of this that accordeth to thee and what ever thing thou wilt under the ascension of the nativity of the man if thou knowest it or under the interrogation of him. thou shalt name by the open name of the man ☉ either for the name of him wch we useth more. and thou shalt fynde forme the ascendant wth strong fortune. be it not retrograde neither falling nor Combust. And the Lord of the ascendant he be strong and also direct or ~~equall~~even in his course in some of his dignityes, and the 10 Lord be he ioyned of the third or vi[th] beholding making him fortunate, and the 10 Lord be he that is Joyned to the Lord of the ascendant and beholding him. And if it befalleth that the Lord of the Ascendent be in signes comannding and the 10 lord in signes obeying fuse thou or melt thou ☉ under such a condition, when all this verily were p[ro]fitt the king of him shall be inclined to him and he shall love none that he putt before him And he shall finde anents him most place, and he shall come by him to most hono[r]. And he shall gett [73] of his king what ever he will and he shall dread him and he shall be anentis him great and higher then all men he shall be to him and before all men more loved and this worke shall appeare durable and great how long the ☉ shall dure and be kept till death depart him And if thou doest this under the ascension of the 10 signe ☉ properly And after this thou hast made ☉ of the king and thou hast put the question and receiving and all maner condicions after that I have putt or sett, thou hast put thy hand of ☉ decem or ten bounden to his necke The king may not let him w[th]out and end. And if he suffereth of him all thing that he may suffer. And if he taketh away from him all thing that he dreadeth of him if God will.

Cu volueris facere ☉ *ad amore &[c]*
When thou wilt make ☉ or working to love thou shalt begin betwixt twayne of them w[ch] thou wilt figure and concord in the day of ♃ under thascension of the nativity of them if thou knowest it or under thascension of Interrogacon of them. And thou shalt name ☉ wth his open name and thou shalt forme thascendent and the 10, and thou shalt make the evill absent from thascendant. And the 11 thou shalt put Lord of Planetts for thou shalt make fortune for him wth the lord of horoscope that is of the ascendant to be ioyned of the lord or sixt beholding and it shall receive him in this maner. Thou shalt fuse ☉ after this thou shalt fuse another ☉ and thou shalt name it by the mname of hum whome thou wilt accord or be bowed fusing it under the 10 ascension from the first ascendant and if there were [73V] the husband of the wife under the 7 ascension And then also wth medling betwixt the Lord of the thing and the figure that thou usest. And put thou the signification of the ascendant w[ch] thou wilt be bowed ioyned to the significato[r] of the first ascendant and if there were betwixt them receiving after that it went before of the condicion of a ☉ p[rd] that is of the first worching evenly, and when the second worching were profitt youre thou or eyther put thou therface of ☉ 2[us] that is of the second worke downeward of the first worke And when this is done in what ever place he were thou shalt

put them wth him And wrap thou them in a Cleane cloth and put thou them in the place where the Lord of the first worke is wch if he were in Journeyes, that is if he go away oft from his house put thou them wth him And when thou hast done this after as I have ordeyned to the nighest to the getting of them wch he will accord of God will and they shall be accorded The mastry sothely of the worke is made in the sothenes of thascendent and wth strength of them wth fortunes and wth absence of evils from it And in healthes of Coniunction & of reception and condition before going. example of wch thing if thou wilt make ☉ to a woman anentis her husband thou shalt make the signification of the 7 to be ioyned wth the Lord of horoscopi [74] And when thou wilt depart or sever twayne thou shalt do in the Contrary of the worke before going in composition and this is ensample of worching by the wch it ought to be wrought

When thou wilt yeld a man of his king hatefull so that he receive him not. Or that how long it shall be kept the ☉ or working Do this that thou make the similitude of him under the ascension of the nativity of him if thou knowest it or under the ascension of Interrogacon of him. And then grave thou ☉ wth his open name. And thou shalt make thascendent infortunate and the 10 wth strong evill. And thou shalt make the Lord of thascendent infortunate by the 10 Lord of opposition if it may be done or of the 4th beholding And be there not betwixt them receiving. And thou shalt make the fortunes to fall from it both from thascendent and from the 10. And when thou hast done this thou shalt grave in the ridge [rim] of ☉ twey names if it were to death grave in the middle of ☉ names before ffurthermore thou shalt grave ☉ in the first habitacle under the signe infortunate wth Canda draconis or wth strong evill. And when thou hast done they shall not accord wthout end. And the kyng shall not to him how long the ☉ were kept And if thou wilt that this worke be stronger put the Lord of thascendent severed from the 10 lord and be he letted from yt And Joyned to the Lord of the house of death and be he letted of yt either by $o - o$ or $o - o$ And when thou hast done this wisely wth the Condition his kyng shall stea him of much hate

[74^v]
And know thou that these worchings raigneth in all worches and things wth the sonnes of Adam useth of profitt and ympediment health & sicknes love and hate, gift & prohibition or letting standing or p^{er}egrination, dispersion or beasts letting and collection of the same, when he that worketh were wyse in such works of planetts Therfore keepe thou those that be of the termes of planetts and of the hid treasures of wisedome And this is the more wisedome

wch God would make open to his servants to getting and p^rofitt of realms to hm be glory into worlds.

Sic facies œ ☉ accipies 2os lapides &^c
Thus thou shalt make eche worching Take twey stones nesh of such quantity as thou shalt make great or little, and thou shalt frot them togither wisely till the facies of them be cleped & Joyned evenly and most certainly After this thou shalt beginne to grave ☉ delving in the nether stone ☉ the head afterward the necke of him, and thou all the body till ☉ be delvyn wth all his utter members And in the other stone thou shallt do also and when the hower were nigh thou shalt Joyne eu eyther, that is to say, thou shalt effuse ☉ wch thou wilt make anon wth Condicon in the prop^er hower what ever sothely were of the worke of ☉ as bynding of [75] scorpions and of other beasts. Thou shalt not charge or care what eu hower thou shalt beginne. And understand thou the fortunes of them that I have expounded to the And if thou followest the order thou shalt finde effect thaked be God Amen

Within of the doomes or Judgem^ts of Hermes of Introduction of this worke he willed them from it And Bolemus said the exposito^r of this booke it behoveth him that search this science that is of worchings and behold the intencion of it, and keepe he and Consider the disposition of it, and do he all things that be in it, ffor it is sothely the science of God all their highest And it behoveth that what ever were done of it be done in his tyem in the day and howers that the power of it be Consydered. Therfore Consider thou it by the Comanndement of God of this

Cu volueris facere aliqua ☉ divide terra &^c
When thou wylt make any op^eration or working divide thou the earth wth his p^arty ffor to everiche of them be names by wch they be formed And upon wch the quantity of them by the will of God be ordeyned Another said Consider thou the fortune of Luna and in infortune of her and the names of Angells in the 4 quarters or Corners of all wilde beasts letting and the lettings of them from the letting of men and of saints and of beasts. And therefore when thou wilt [75^V] make invocation by wch thou wouldst lett from the impediment wth the p^arty of the day if it were thy worke or wth the p^arty of the night if it were in the might w^ththe name of all angels wch serveth to the p^arty of this wch thou seechest Do thou understand it, and know thou best the names of them to the first p^arty. and the names of the kinde wch thou wilt figure as a locust or lice or wilde beasts or reptiles or haile or lightning or other such as these wth wch thou makest that thou take away from them impediments.

These be the names of Angels serving to the first pᵃʳty therefore clepe thou by them hit that thou wylt Cemeyl. Ameyl. hoasaresin   And enclepe thou by the mastery of them aurafedyn and the name of the head og signes ameyeyl. arfeyl. et. dabril. And the name of the head of all the names aritereinhin

The names of Angells that serveth to the second pᵃʳty Barcayl. durayl. And the head of all the names Celaban alatar. The names of signes and of angels that serve to the signes and the mastry of them is Balgathoaith

And the names of signes and of Angels serving to the 4ᵗʰ pᵃʳty Dareyl. badadeyl. abrayel. And the names that be before the nights. When therefore thou wilt or wilnes anything enclepe thou the 4 pᵃʳts of the yeere, and thou shalt gett thy thing if God will.

[76]
And these be the name of the 4 tymes of the yeere The first Etharthea and the beginning of the yeere from the moneth of October The second pᵃʳty Althen The third gᵘmen. And the 4ᵗʰ of the yeere is ended furab.

Names wᵗʰ wᶜʰ Sol is cleped in the 4ᵗʰ pᵃʳtyes. In the first pᵃʳty Arbiamyn. In the second pᵃʳty Abhermoyn In the third pᵃʳty Abtororyn. In the 4ᵗʰ pᵃʳty Ganynydin The pᵃʳtyes of Solis in the first Aries ♉ & ♊ In the second ♋ ♌ & ♍. In the third pᵃʳty ♎ ♏ and ♐ In the 4ᵗʰ pᵃʳty ♑ ♒ & ♓.

The names of ☽ in the 4 pᵃʳrtyes of the yeere. It is Cleped in the first pᵃʳty Labrayon. In the second pᵃʳty Aliaztay uenym. In the third pᵃʳty Abraoryn And in the 4ᵗʰ pᵃʳty Barianyn.

The names of the heavens in each party of the yeere be these. It is named in the first pᵃʳty of the yeere hirinitiz. In the third Maaza cetad In the fourth Tenfat.

The names of the Earth in the 4 pᵃʳtyes of the yeere It is nempned in the first pᵃʳty Cemaaton. In the Second Haysamyn. the Interᵖretation of wᶜʰ is Aliebingie i- sicca that is Dry. And in the third pᵃʳty Henayenyn. And in another booke tabilyn. And in the fourth Heymaryn habyrehin. And after another booke in the fourth fadnathin.

The names of the Southern windes in the 4 pᵃʳtyes of the yeere. It is cleped in the first pᵃʳty Nimhe In the second pᵃʳty bardaglie. In the third Laathedin and if thou wilt Zaholodin. And in the 4th gaafonyn or Zimariz. And in the 4th p^arty dermaryn.

[76^v]
The names of the Northerne wyndes in the 4 p^arts of the yeere It is cleped in the first p^arty Menzurnyn and in the second Messelyn. And in the third Lemhocri.

These be the names in the earth in wch be divided the tymes of the yeeres the moneths and dayes. The names of the sea in the 4 p^arts of the yeere. In the first Alamyn. In the second mohoromyn. In the third yeytelbylblyn. In the fourth party Meleadea.

Cu volueris ut benedicat tibj Deus &^c
when thou wilt that God blesse to thee in fishing and fishes be multiplied be the comanndement of God write thou the name of the sea wth the p^artyes and make ☉ to thesimilitude of water and let it be in the part of the water wch thou wilt for the fishes will be multiplied by the Comanndement of God in it how long ☉ dureth and over that by the helpe of it and vertue.

Cu volueris necare feras impedientes &^c
When thou wilt slea wilde beasts letting rayse thy hands to heaven tourning thy face towards the sonne of it were day. In the night sothely against the moone. And say the name of the sonne and the name of the moone in the p^artyes of them of the p^artyes of the yeere. and enclepe thou the 7 names by wch God made the 7 dayes, for thou shalt slea wylde beasts letting of trees of sheepe of kyne and other like beasts. Thou shalt slea also Locusts and wormes [77] of Cornes. Say therefore the 7 names by wch God alhighest fromed eache Creature and these be the names laharmyn. lahelagin. liglayaforyn tayal. ganary. chinlaiasalin. These sothely be the names wth wch thou shalt clepe wylde beasts or fowles letting. And by these glorious names wth wch Moyses the prophet. And thou shalt say *Dico tibi O fera aut avis ut recedes a finibus huius civitatis vel villa quo voluit creator noster et diu duraverit hæc noia scripta vel ☉* That is to say to thee O thou wilde beast or byrde that do passé away from the ends of this city or towne whether that o^ur Creator will, and entreth he not into them till into the world, neither lett ye how long these names dureth written or ☉

Cu volueris qualecuq specie de avibus &^c
When thou wylt that every kinde of foules and wylde beasts and all beasts

and what ev^r place thou wilt gather, if thou wilt that they be multiplied there be there a blessing. Say wth and highe voyce and enclepe by these names thou shalt say *Avis per nomen tuu invoco te O avis munda qua mundavit tuns creator audi q dico tibj per 7 noia sanctificata et dices per virtutem ejus qui ducit sole inter æthera cælj hoc est in medio cælj. et per noia obedientes estote et redite ad habitacula vra et generate et multiplicaminj in sæcula sæculor* That is to say This fowle whome thy Creator hath made clean, heare [77^V] thou that I say to thee by the 7 names hallowed And thou shalt say by the vertue of him that leadeth the sonne amongst the heavens, that is in the middle of heaven and by these names be ye obedient and come yo^u agayne to yo^{ur} habitacles multiplied into worlds of worlds.

When thou wilt that the same appeare to thee openly enclepe thou the name of the sonne in the p^{arty} wch thou were as I have expounded to thee in the beginning of the booke And the name of God ffor the sonne shall uncover to thee, and thou shalt behold the being of it, and what ever thou axest it shall be given to thee in the same hower, and thou shalt say Maryeyl.

When thou wilt that fyer be quenched & burne not write 7 names before it shall be quenched by the Comanndement of God Malcheyl. sedlayeyy Amyamya. Crediatil. norzayeyl. Bardaeyl. Thou shalt say by the walles of the sonne it shall be quenched by the Comanndement of God.

And when thou wylt bynde tongs that they let not thee inclepe thou before them while the be onterp^{reted} these names wch be 7. Selateyl. lahleyl. maynaceyl. By these p^{recious} names yo^u and all yo^{urs} I have destroyed yo^u by the vertue of God Hyeydy. and there hath hallowed yo^u Ancyim ualayeyl. Uassalyil

When thou wilt knowe what is to come in the yeere make cleane thy self of all thy trespasses [78] and meeke thee to God and all good works and axe thou not any thing wthout his hower and trowe thou sothely and doubt thou not in it And if it taryrth it shall be shewed to thee in steepes.

Liber Lunæ

Dixit Bolemus phs de hijs quæ pº neccia sunt &c
Bolemus the pher said of these that first be necessary the names of dayes and of night of howers when it is necessary to pray by them and to seche helpe by the natures of them for strength of them by the Comanndement of God.

Knowe thou therefore that the first of howers of everiche day is nempned Vehich, in it men pray to their Creatoʳ and it is able to bynding of all things

The second hower is names yeror. In it Angells pray their Creatoʳ, and in this hower be made the worchings of love and of concord betweene all maner Creatures and men and coniunction of spirits

The third is named Ansur. In it fowles do thankes to their Creatoʳ. In this be made the worchings of fishes and of all fowles.

The fourth is named Oelgil. In it Creature do thanks to their Creatoʳ. In it be made the worchings of serpents of scorpions and of Dragons.

The fifth is named Coaleth In it all beasts do thanks to their Creatoʳ. In it be made the worchings of wolves of cattes and of all wylde beasts.

The sixth is names Coulher In it prayeth Cherubin for the synnes of men. In it be made the worchings of Becends and of men to be delivered.

The seventh is named Jador In it prayeth Seraphin [78ᵛ] bearing the throne. In it be made the workings of concord betwixt kings.

The eight is named Jasumah. In it be made worchings betwixt men.

The ixᵗʰ is named Luron. In it is made worchings of them that goeth a pilgrimage least theeves let them neither go tou to them wᵗʰout end.

The xᵗʰ is named Sahon. In it water singeth to his Lord. In it descendeth the spirit of God, and it maketh ighen to quake. In it be made worchings taking kings when any man entreth to them that they speake not evill to him. And of water ber taken the same hower and medled to an ointment hallowed, and eche that suffreth a wicked spirit were annoynted he shall be healed by the Comanndement of God.

The eleventh is named Relimj Init Just men be glad. In it be made the worchings of love and of Concord and of dilection

The xiiᵗʰ is named Vahialon. In it is made merciablenes of men. In it be made workings of silence that he speake not wᵗʰout end upon whome' this worke were.

The names of the howere of ye night in wch worchings made be more worth and more mighty then the working of the day by much.

The first hower is nempned Hamon wch I found in another diacholym. In it is made the orison of divels to their Creato^r and they lett no man till they be raised from the Orison And in this hower be made the worchings of sylence.

[79]

The second is name Canbeul. In this hower be made the worching of fishes and of water leches and of Crocdiles and of froggs and of all water beasts that they be not moved

The third is named Thabor in it singeth beasts in it be made worchings that fire burne not and of dragons and serpents that they lett not And in it is bounden eache long that it speake not.

The fourth is named Alahan. In it were divells upon sepulchers, of this is made dread and if a man offendeth or graveth them he shall dread and the haires of him shalbe raised and quaking he shall dread from them. And in this hower be made worchings that be graven in gold and silver and concord and love in croco and rubeo that is in saffron & red and of all Impediment and evill.

The fifth is named Camifer In it goeth water and Creatures singeth. In it be made workings of evill clouds and of huge wyndes.

The sixth is nempned Zaron. In it resteth the water and is ceased, and if there were ravished of it in the same hower and medled to the oyntmt of priests hallowed, and they that have fevers were annoynted wth it wch sleepeth not sound sleepe and rest by the Comandmt of God. In it be made the worchings of Dreames by wch it shall be seene in dreames what is to be done in good and evill.

The 7th is nempned Cafor in it be made the [79^V] worchings of kings that who ever axeth any thing of them and they letteth him not, and they should not deny any thing w^{th}out end by the Comandement of God.

The viii^{th} is named Cinach. In it seeds of the earth prayeth the highest God. In it be made the worchings of meads and of gardens and of trees, and of all maner seeds of the earth that they be abled and kept from all Impediments by the sufferance of God.

The ix^{th} is named Oroostafar. In it be made workings of Angels to the Lord of worlds. and in it be made the workings of ingoings to kings and of buildings, the tongues of men and the other Creatures and of away putting the Impediment of them.

Th x[th] is named Malho. And it is profitable in it to be made workings that a woman do not fornication or women of all a region

The xi[th] is named Alaacho. In it be opened the gates of heaven w[th] orisons who ever enclepeth his Lord God shall give that he axeth. In it be made the worchings of most concord and of love durable to weddings &[c] And it in it be smitten togither the wings of fowles and of Cocks whereof it is named Aalaco And it is of all the over p[ar]ty of the earth And in it waxeth the sonne upon the Creature of God of the high Paradice.

The xii[th] is named fellen In this hower resteth the hoast of heavens light gives while men praseth their highst Creato[r]. And in it be made the workings of silence and of religion. And it is cleped the worke [80] of stonyng and of gastenes who that beholdeth it amased and astonyed as a man out of wytt he is troubled and he may not speake. And that that were done in this hower of worke shall not be losed of any man wth out end, and this now is proved. There be made sothely 4 Sutyl. tynnyn. sylverii and ~~Bas~~ Brassyn And nothing may adnull of them any thing of the fyrst and the last.

Cu volueris ligare latrines vt non &[c]
When thou wylt bynde theeves that they enter not into any house when the first face were of Alhamel that is to say Ariets ascendant and Luna make the ymage of a man of brasse And when thymage were p[ar]fite or fulfilled then say thou *Alligo œm latrine ab hac domo per hanc* ☉ And bury it in the middle of the house and he shall not enter w[th]out end.

That kyne dwell still upon calves under the same horoscope That is under the first face of ♈ and Luna in the same ascendant make ☉ of a calf of brasse saying *Ligo œm vacca p hanc* ☉ *vt qu enq super ea transierit non recedat.* Be it burned where thou wylt.

That fyer tende or kindle not under the same horoscope make ☉ of a man Coprin or of Copper the head of w[ch] be upon the head of an Hounde w[th] w[ch] be a candlesticke saying *Ligovi igno ab hac domo vt non accentdat[or] in ea in æterna* that it be not tende or kindle in it w[th]out end Be it buried at thy liking.

[80[V]]

That a woman sit kemyng her head under the same horoscope make ☉ of copper holding in her hand a Combe saying *Non transeat sup[er] istam imagine mulier quin sedeat pecteuscaput sum* That is to say Ne passe thou not upon this Image a woman that ne she sit kemyng her head Be it buryed at thy liking in the way in wch they passe ffor there shall not passe a woman that ne shall discover her head frotting it that her haires fall ffor to bynde serpents Under the same horoscope being the second face of Alkebs that is to say Ariets ascending make ☉ of a serpent brazen or of brasse saying I have bound eche serpent that in this place they let no man or this *Ligavi œm serpente^s vt in isto loco neiem impediant.* Be it buried in the middle place divided.

That the members of a man be bound under the same horoscope being the third face of Alhamel ascending of brasse ☉ of a man upright saying *Ligavi te Socrate^s seu fronicu^s vt cu aliqua coire non possis* That is to say I have bound thee Socrates or fronicus that wth any thou go not togither or might not go togither, be it buried in a dry pitt.

That a man have fever Under the same horoscope being the third face of Alhamel ascending that to whome thou wilt fevers take, be there graven ☉ an ymage of a man in a plate of tynne wth this orison. *sicut es figura* ☉ *Socratis seu ironici sic accipiant eu febres vel demones* that is to say As thou art the figure of worching [81] of Socrates or fronicus so take him fevers or divels In the sea of water it is to be buried.

That an enemy enter not in a City. Under the first face to Taurus horoscope being make ☉ of a man having a sword in the hand in the first face of the hower being saying *Ligavi hanc Civitate vt non expuguet eam inimicus in æternu neg exercitus.* That is to say I have bound this City that an ememy fight not against it w^thout end neither an hoast. And then be it buried in the 4 p^arts of the City in the middle of the same.

That locke open. Under the second face of Taurus ^being^ horoscopo ~~being~~ that Solution be made of locke Iron saying *Solvo seras tactas cu* ☉ *ista.* That is to say I loose locke touched w_th this worching. And standing the locke shall be opened.

That hounds barke not Under the 3 face of ♉ the hower being make ♉ of an hounde of lead, and have he it wth him, and go he surely among hounds.

That an horse stand. Under the third face of ♉ make ☉ of an horse of lead Saying *non transeat super istam figura equus quin stet.* That is to say Ne passé there not upon this figure an horse that ne he stand, and be it buried at thy liking in the third face of ♉

That a minstrell be distrayned under the [81^V] second face of ♊ the hower being make ☉ of a man of waxe or of brasse some instrum^t holding saying

Non canat Joculator vbi hæc ☉ fuerit quin disfruant[e] ejus instrumenta duc inter eos
That is to say Ne sing not a minstrell where this worching were that ne instruments of him be destroyed, led betwixts them.

Ut hortus non faciat fructu sub eode &[c]

That a gardeine make not fruit. Under the same make ☉ of a tree upon wch be ☉ of a serpent of Copper. About the serpent be there wormes saying *Ligavi hunc hortu vt fructu non faciat* That is to say I have bound this garden that it make not fruite. Andbe it buried in the garden and wormes shall eat all.

That whome thou lovest follow thee. [1]Under the second face of Cancer the hower being make ☉ of a woman of Tyme or waxe saying *Attraxi cor N fil: mris ad ineipsu propter amore et dilectionem et provocavi spni ejus provocatione forti vt meus ignis et ejus virtus et sicut proocatione venti et ejus ffatus.* Touche whome thou lovest and she shall follow thee obeying to thee If not hang it in an high tree, and thou shalt see marvells And blowe ☉ when thou seeth these.

That a wall fall Under the third face of Cancer the hower being make a wall of lead saying [82] *Cadat ois paries apud quem sepeliatur ista ☉ et cadet iste sub que sepeliat[r]* That is to say eche wlall fall anentis the w[ch] this ☉ is buried. And this shall fall under w[ch] this is buried.

That haile fall not. Under the 3 face of Cancer the hower ascending make ☉ of a wenche all in lead, in the hand of whome be haile saying *Non transeat super ☉ ista grando loco vbi fuerit sepulta et non cadet ibi grando* That is to say ne passe there not upon the ☉ haile in the place where it were buried at thy liking.

That a man be made sicle. Under the second face of Leo the hower being make ☉ of a man of brasse or tynne raising his hands saying *Pro qualibel infirmitate accipiat N fil: N mris febris vel quævis infirmitas deinde in pelago subhumetur.* That is to say ffor each infirmity take the son of N. of N. mother fevers of what sicknes thou wylt. And then be it buried in the sea, or be it put under the treen betill of a better and say to the heat that dolor and heate take the head og him.

That a field bring not fruite Under the first face of Virgo, the hower being

---

[1] In the margin at this place:
   sub 2[a] facie
   ♋[i] *horoscopo*
   existente
   fac opus vel
   Imagine

make ☉ of a woman of tynne or of lead or of earth, and put In his right hand 2 eares of Corne that he hold them saying *Ligavi hunc agru vt non naseatur in eo messis* That is to say I have bound this field that corne waxe not in it, be it buried in the field & it shall never beare fruit of the kynde that is in the hand of yᵉ ymage.

[82ᵛ]

That ravens be gathered togither. The first face of Virgo the hower being make ☉ of half a raven, and another halve deale under the second face of Virgo saying *Non remaneat Corbus nisi veniat ad hanc* ☉ That is to say Ne remayne there not a raven but he come to this ☉ or ymage Be it buried to thy liking.

That a shepe stand. Under the third face of Virgo ascending the hower being make ☉ of a man of tynne having wᵗʰ him a litle bell saying upon yt. *Nonremaneat Ovis vel Capra transiens super eam quiu stet.* That is to say Ne remayne there not a sheepe or a goate passing upon yt that he ne stand Be he buried at thy liking.

That workemen worke not any thing Under the second face of Virgo make of a man of waxe wᵗʰ so many instruments that thou wilt bynde saying to everich when thou wilt bynde In wᶜʰ place were wont to be done And say that they werche not any thing.

That there be not sold any thing in the tent — In the first face of ♎ ascending make ☉ of a man holding in the hand *libram* saying *Ligavi hoc tentoriu vt abijciat ab eo hoies vt non vendatur aliquio in eo durat* ☉ *hic sepulta* That is to say. I have bound this tent that he cast from him men. That any thing be not sold in yt while ☉ dureth buried heere.

[83]

Ligatio regis pro malo secunda facie Libræ &ᶜ

Bynding of a king for evill In the second face of Libra the hower being make ☉ of a king of lead sitting upon a benche and in environ of him make keepᵉʳˢ saying *Ligavi hunc rege N perista* ☉ *ab hac regione vt non in ea malu faciat neg ererceat in ea injurias.* That is to say I have bound this king N by this ☉ or working from this region that he do not evill in it neither use in ut iniuryes. In the middle of a region or of a city be it buryed.

That thou take fishes In the second face of Libra the hower being make ☉ of a ship of lead full of fishes saying *non remaneat pisces quiu veniat ad hanc* ☉ That is to say Ne remayme there not a fishe that ne he come to this ☉ or working Be it buried in the river.

That a man make himself bare or naked. Under the second face of Scorpius the hower being make ☉ of a man naked of brasse saying *Non transeat super hanc ☉ aliquis quiu proijciat vestimenta sua et nudus remaneat* That is to say Ne passe there not upon this ☉ any manthat he ne cast away his Clothes and remayne bare or naked. Be it buried at thy liking.

That a man or a woman passe not that ne he sing and play, the first face of Capricorne make ☉ of a wenche of tynne In the hand of her be a plate of tynne saying *non transeat super ista* [83ᵛ] ☉ *vir neg mulier quiu cantet et ludat* That is to say Ne passe there not upon this ☉ a man nor a woman that he ne sing and play. Be it buried in the way at thy liking where women passeth.

That flyes fly from an house. Under the second face of Aquarius the howere being make ☉ of a fly in the stone of a ring either of gold or silver and about ☉ these words be written *Non vides musca quæ aderit quavis mille milliu essent locu illu derelinquent et mors configet eis. deinde eo dicente musca moriamini* That is to say thou shalt not see a fly that shall abide although there were a thousand thousand they shall forsake that place and death shall befall to them. And then he saying flyes be ye dead The ring be it discovered in the house and they should fly.

ffor to bynde a taverne or to agast write these names in virgin pᵃʳchement and bynde wᵗʰ a thred of brasse to some post in the taverne. *uriel . hobiel. dodiel uriel daniel kauael salguel michael assiduel duriel conjuro vos angelos fortes vt removeatis œm hoiem q non posset accedere ad Taverna ista ad emendu aliquid in eo. Conjure vos per angelu forte qui a Deo diligitur super œs et est sine fine Amen.* That is to say I coniure yoᵘ strong angels that ne remayne eche man that he may not come nigh to this taverne to buy any thing in it. I coniure yoᵘ by the strong Angell wᶜʰ is loved of God upon all. And he is wᵗʰout end.

BIBLIOGRAPHY

Agrippa, [Heinrich] Cornelius. *De occultia philosophia libri tres*, edited by Vittoria Perrone Compagni. Leiden: E. J. Brill, 1992.

_____ (ed. Skinner, Stephen). *The Fourth Book of Occult Philosophy*. London: Askin Publishers, 1978; REPRINT – Berwick: Ibis Press, 2005.

_____. *Three Books of Occult Philosophy*, translated by James Freake; annotated with modern commentary by Donald Tyson. St. Paul: Llewellyn Publications, 1993.

Barrett, Francis. *The Magus, or Celestial Intelligencer; Being A Complete System of Occult Philosophy*, with a New Introduction by Timothy d'Arch Smith. Secaucus: The Citadel Press, 1967 & 1975 – a reproduction of the 1801 edition (London: Lackington, Allen, and Co.)

Betz, Hans Dieter. *The Greek Magical Papyri in Translation*, VOLUME ONE: TEXTS, second edition. Chicago – London: University of Chicago Press, 1992.

Burnett, Charles. 'Arabic, Greek, and Latin Works on Astrological Magic Attributed to Aristotle,' in *Magic and Divination in the Middle Ages: Texts and Techniques in the Islamic and Christian Worlds* [COLLECTED STUDIES SERIES: CS557]. Aldershot: Variorum, 1996.

Cresswell, Julia. *The Watkins Dictionary of Angels*. London: Watkins Publishing, 2006.

Davies, Owen. *Grimoires: A History of Magic Books*. Oxford: Oxford University Press, 2009.

Gollancz, Hermann (ed.) *Sepher Maphteah Shelomoh (Book of the Key of Solomon): An Exact Facsimile of an Original Book of Magic in Hebrew....* London: Oxford University Press, 1914; REPRINT with a foreword by Stephen Skinner, York Beach: Teitan Press, 2008.

Herrmann, Klaus. 'The Reception of Hekhalot-Literature in Yohanan Alemanno's Autograph Paris MS 849,' in *Studies in Jewish Manuscripts*, edited by Joseph Dan and Klaus Herrmann. Tübingen: Mohr Siebeck, 1999.

Idel, Moshe. 'Hermeticism and Judaism,' in *Hermeticism and the Renaissance: Intellectual History and the Occult in the Early Modern Europe*, edited by

Ingrid Merkel and Allen G. Debus. Washington: Folger Books, 1988.

_____. 'On European Cultural Renaissances and Jewish Mysticism,' in *Kabbalah: Journal for the Study of Jewish Mystical Texts*, VOLUME 13, edited by Daniel Abrams and Avraham Elqayam (Los Angeles: Cherub Press, 2005.

Karr, Don (ed). *Solomonic Magic*, online at HERMETIC KABBALAH, maintained by Colin Low: www.digital-brilliance.com/contributed/Karr/Solomon/index.php

Karr, Don; and Skinner, Stephen (eds). *Sepher Raziel – Liber Salomonis: A 1564 English Grimoire from Sloane MS 3826*. Singapore: Golden Hoard Press, 2010.

Kieckhefer, Richard. *Forbidden Rites: A Necromancer's Manual of the Fifteenth Century*. University Park: Pennsylvania State University Press, 1997.

_____. *Magic in the Middle Ages* [CAMBRIDGE MEDIEVAL TEXTBOOKS]. Cambridge: Cambridge University Press, 1989.

Klaassen, Frank. 'English Manuscripts of Magic, 1300-1500: A Preliminary Survey,' in *Conjuring Spirits: Texts and Traditions of Medieval Ritual Magic*, edited by Claire Fanger. University Park: Pennsylvania State University Press, 1998.

_____. *Religion, Science, and the Transformations of Magic: Manuscripts of Magic 1300-1600*. PhD dissertation, University of Toronto, 1999.

Láng, Benedek. *Unlocked Books: Manuscripts of Learned Magic in the Medieval Libraries of Central Europe*. University Park: Pennsylvania State University Press, 2008.

Lelli, Fabrizio. 'Hermes among the Jews: Hermetica as Hebraica: From Antiquity to the Renaissance,' in *Magic, Ritual, and Witchcraft*, Volume 2, Number 2. Philadelphia: University of Pennsylvania Press, Winter 2007.

Lidaka, Juris. 'The Book of Angels, Rings, Characters and Images of the Planets: Attributed to Osbern Bokenham,' in *Conjuring Spirits: Texts and Traditions of Medieval Ritual Magic*, edited by Claire Fanger. University Park: Pennsylvania State University Press, 1998.

Maddison, Francis, and Turner, Anthony. 'The Names and Faces of the Hours,' in *Between Demonstration and Imagination: Essays in the History of Science and Philosophy Presented to John D. North*, edited by Lodi

Nauta and Arjo Vanderjagt. Leiden: Brill, 1999.

Mathers, S. Liddell MacGregor (ed). *The Key of Solomon*. London: Redway, 1909; REPRINT – New York: Samuel Weiser, Inc., 1974.

McLean, Adam (ed). *A Treatise on Angel Magic* [MAGNUM OPUS HERMETIC SOURCEWORKS, # 15]. Edinburgh: Magnum Opus Sourceworks, 1982; REPRINT – Grand Rapids: Phanes Press, 1990; REPRINT – York Beach: Weiser Books, 2006.

Page, Sophie. *Magic in Medieval Manuscripts*. Toronto: University of Toronto Press, 2004.

Peterson, Joseph H. (ed). "A. W. Greenup: Sefer ha Levanah," at TWILIT GROTTO > www.esotericarchives.com/levanah/levanah.htm; also on the *Esoteric Archives* CD (Kasson: Twilit Grotto, 2000 & 2008) — available at www.esotericarchives.com/cd.htm

_____ (ed). *The Lesser Key of Solomon*. York Beach: Weiser Books, 2001.

Picatrix: The Classic Medieval Handbook of Astrological Magic, translated [from the Latin] by John Michael Greer and Christopher Warnock. Iowa City: Adocentyn Press, 2010.

Picatrix: Ghayat al Hakim – The Goal of the Wise, VOLUME I, translated from the Arabic by Hashem Atallah, edited by William Kiesel. Seattle: Ouroboros Press, 2000.

Picatrix: Ghayat al Hakim – The Goal of the Wise, VOLUME II, translated from the Arabic by Hashem Atallah and Geylan Holmquest, edited by William Kiesel. Seattle: Ouroboros Press, 2008.

Sangerman, Robert. *Jewish Translation History: A Bibliography of Bibliographies and Studies*. Amsterdam/Philadelphia: John Benjamins, 2002.

Skinner, Stephen. *The Complete Magician's Tables*. Singapore: Golden Hoard Press, 2006.

Skinner, Stephen. *Techniques of Graeco-Egyptian Magic*. Singapore: Golden Hoard Press, 2014.

Skinner, Stephen. *Techniques of Solomonic Magic*. Singapore: Golden Hoard Press, 2015.

Skinner, Stephen; and Rankine, David (eds). *The Goetia of Dr Rudd*. London – Singapore: Golden Hoard Press, 2007.

Thorndike, Lynn. *A History of Magic and Experimental Science*, VOLUME II. New

York – London: Columbia University Press, 1923.

Torijano, Pablo A. *Solomon the Esoteric King: From King to Magus, Development of a Tradition.* Leiden: Brill, 2002.

Waite. Arthur Edward. *Book of Ceremonial Magic Including the Rites and Mysteries of Goetic Theurgy, Sorcery and Infernal Necromancy.* London: William Rider, 1911 — reprinted frequently.

Warnock, Christopher. "Mansions of the Moon in Astrology & Magic" at RENAISSANCE ASTROLOGY >

www.renaissanceastrology.com/mansionsmoon.html

_____. "Planetary Hours & Days Main Page," at RENAISSANCE ASTROLOGY >www.renaissanceastrology.com/planetaryhoursarticle.html

_____. *The Mansions of the Moon: A Lunar Zodiac for Astrology and Magic.* Iowa City: Renaissance Astrology, 2010.

Index

Made in the USA
Las Vegas, NV
16 January 2024